Printed ephemera

COLLECTION ORGANISATION AND ACCESS

Printed ephemera

COLLECTION ORGANISATION AND ACCESS

Alan Clinton BA PhD

CLIVE BINGLEY LONDON

FIRST PUBLISHED 1981 BY CLIVE BINGLEY LTD
16 PEMBRIDGE ROAD LONDON W11

SET IN 10 ON 11 POINT PRESS ROMAN BY ALLSET
PRINTED AND BOUND IN THE UK BY
REDWOOD BURN LIMITED TROWBRIDGE AND ESHER
COPYRIGHT © ALAN CLINTON 1981
ALL RIGHTS RESERVED
CLIVE BINGLEY ISBN: 0-85157-337-1

British Library Cataloguing in Publication Data

Clinton, Alan
    Printed ephemera.
    1. Printed ephemera
    I. Title
    001.55'2024092   NC1280

    ISBN 0-85157-337-1

CONTENTS

PREFACE

The aim of this book is to investigate an important problem faced by
all those who organise printed sources of knowledge. Traditionally
librarians deal with books, museum curators with artifacts, and
archivists with manuscripts. Yet at the edges of what was once regarded
as the proper concern of each of these are large amounts of printed
paper. These materials are often designated nowadays as 'ephemera',
and are generally distinguished by being difficult to arrange and to
find.

Since the term came into general use in the early 1960s, a number of
publications have appeared giving examples of the various forms of
printed ephemera and describing the location of such material in
particular fields. The Dainton Committee on National Libraries in
1969 maintained that the new centralised library structure it helped to
bring into being should take account of the 'great quantity and variety
of ephemeral material', especially in the social sciences. (Report of the
National Libraries Committee, Cmnd 4028 p76). In 1971, Mr J.E.
Pemberton, in a report referred to many times in the following pages,
put forward proposals for doing this through a National Documents
Library. Two conferences sponsored by the Aslib Social Science
Group followed, and a Working Party within the British Library Reference Division discussed the problem in the mid 1970s. However, no
concrete results followed.

This was not because of any diminution of interest in the topic of
printed ephemera. There was a great expansion in the sphere of private
collection, and in 1975 the Ephemera Society was set up. During the
1970s there was a veritable explosion in the technology of information
provision and in attitudes towards how it should be dispensed. In the
museum world there has been a growth in centralised and computer
based retrieval techniques, particularly through the work of the Museum
Documentation Association. In the world of archives there has been a
steady improvement in means of granting access to material. There
have been similar changes in librarianship, reflected in the attitudes of

7

a new generation determined to use any means to improve information provision to the widest possible community.

A further step in the direction of discussing the problems of printed ephemera was taken in November 1977 at a meeting sponsored by the Standing Conference for Local History and the Local History Group of the Library Association. This established the Advisory Committee on Ephemera and Minor Publications (alias ADCEMP) with Mr Julian Roberts, Keeper of Printed Books at the Bodleian Library, as Chairman and Miss Dorothy McCulla, Librarian of the Local Studies Library at the Birmingham City Library, as Secretary. This Committee worked on various definitions and proposals in the field, which are referred to in Chapter One below. During 1978 further discussions began between the British Library Research and Development Department and the Bodleian Library Oxford about how best to develop the study of the problem. It was then decided to found a project under the headship of Mr Michael Turner, Head of Conservation at the Bodleian Library and well known for bringing the famous John Johnson Collection into the Bodleian. The project was given the title the 'Preliminary Survey of Collections of Ephemera'. The survey was carried out by the present author during 1979 and the early part of 1980, and this book is one of the results.

The particular form assumed by the present study thus derives from the many discussions which brought it about. Its central concern is to look at ephemeral printed materials where they are and to see how they are arranged. This may not be what the interested reader expects, nor does it necessarily correspond to the preconceptions of the author. However, it is hoped that by setting out the manifold form and organisation of non-book printed materials it will be possible to push forward knowledge in this field, and as a result to refine and develop solutions to the problems that have been discussed over the years.

The main approach adopted in this book to the problems posed by non-book printed materials is to examine the form and management of collections of such materials, in the arts and social sciences. Three topics have been chosen, less for their specific content than for the range of their subject matter. Much of the book (Chapters Three, Five and Seven as well as Appendices Two, Three, Five and Seven) is devoted to giving details of collections including non-book printed materials in the chosen fields. The purpose of the other chapters is to outline some of the general conclusions that have been arrived at as a result of examining collections that include printed ephemera, and to suggest means whereby access and organisation might be improved, both within individual collections and on a national scale. From the particular vantage point at the edge of various professional activities, it has been possible to consider such matters as levels of cataloguing and forms of access in ways that may not always occur to those who have particular concerns.

In this way Chapter Four deals with some of the problems both of private collectors and of custodians of public archives, as well as with relations between them, for which it aims to suggest improvements. Chapter Six discusses some current methods of cataloguing images and how they might be expanded. This is supplemented in Appendix Six by a list of some of the picture collections studied in pursuance of this theme. Chapter Seven, in order to set out the materials necessary for the study of the current social problem which has been chosen, discusses more generally the world of information provision and recent developments in such fields as community librarianship. Chapter Eight goes on to deal with some general problems of the relationship between governmental authorities, pressure groups and others operating in the field. Chapter Nine summarises some of these particular conclusions, and sets out the case for a National Register of Collections.

One specific problem has to be faced from the start, and it is discussed at some length in Chapter One. This derives from the lack of precision in the term 'ephemera' and the great variety of attitude to its meaning and use. Where some see only single sheets of paper, others see large bulky documents and reports. Any effort at precise delineation of ephemeral printed materials broke down as they were looked at. This is the justification of the approach through collections rather than ephemera itself, and for the thematic perspective which dominates this book. Appendix Four gives some examples of places where this logic has been accepted also. This is not to say that there do not exist general ephemera collections, and a number of them are listed and discussed in Chapter Two and Appendix One.

This book sets out more details on ephemeral printed materials than any other known to the author. It discusses the issues which have been encountered in looking at ephemeral printed material in a very wide variety of settings and contexts. Generally speaking, it agrees with the conclusions of those who have previously studied the subject, notably in supporting the establishment of a National Register of Collections. The arguments for such a register are given in Chapter Nine, along with suggestions of how it might work. For reasons also explained there, it has not proved possible to produce any measure of output of ephemeral printed materials. Nor could any particular methodology for further work in the field be proposed when the methods already applied are as varied as the forms of communication and research. However, it is assumed that such further work ought to aim at producing surveys and registers rather than fixed directories, along the same general lines that have been employed here.

A work of this kind would have been impossible without the author incurring a wide range of debts. As an outsider in most of the worlds which were entered in the course of constructing this book, I naturally relied a great deal on the patience and tolerance of many hundreds of individuals who responded to my questions, however ignorant and incomprehending my enquiries seemed. In particular I owe a great deal to numerous people in every single division of the British Library, of the Bodleian Library, Cambridge University Library and the national libraries of Scotland and Wales. Although Mr Michael Turner, Head of Conservation at the Bodleian Library has simply regarded himself as taking the role of supervisor of the project, his extensive knowledge of the issues involved has provided virtually every starting point, and his excellent advice, even where it has not been taken, has served to mould every conclusion.

The Advisory Committee on Ephemera and Minor Publications, whose formation has already been mentioned, played an important role not only in the form taken by this project, but also in its subsequent development. Besides these members of the Committee whose advice is mentioned in other contexts, I would like to refer to the contributions of Mr Maurice Rickards of the Ephemera Society and Mr H.V. Radcliffe of the Newark District Museum. Also important was the advice of those who were working on related projects. I should mention in particular the 'Investigation of Local Publications' at Loughborough University conducted by Mr Paul Sturges and Miss Diana Dixon with the help of Miss K. Mowle. This proceeded in close parallel with the present project, which has benefitted greatly from numerous discussions on common concerns. There was also value in discussion with the project on access to local government documentation undertaken by Mr Don Kennington of Capital Planning Information Limited, and the survey of organisation and control of local government documentation of Mr Barry Nuttall, Sub-Librarian of the Leeds Polytechnic. I am also grateful to those involved in 'the Management of Community Information Resources and Ephemeral Publication' carried out at the Leeds Polytechnic School of Librarianship, and to the Community Information Project based in the Library Association.

The main conclusions of the project were discussed as a result of papers given to a number of audiences in mid-1980. The first of these was a British Library Humanities Information Research Seminar held in Sheffield on 28th-30th March. Another seminar, on Access to Local Government Information was held on 12th-13th June at the Dunchurch College of Management and run by Capital Planning Information. I also met the Aslib Social Science Group on 23rd June. There was also a seminar to discuss the conclusions of this project together with the 'Investigation of Local Publications' of Paul Sturges and Diana Dixon held

10

at Loughborough University on 10th-11th July. I am most grateful to all who participated in these discussions, in particular to those whose good advice I have not taken.

From the world of archives, I owe a particular debt of gratitude to Mr Richard Storey, Archivist at the Modern Record Centre, University of Warwick, and to Mr W.J. Serjeant, County Archivist, Suffolk Record Office and sometime President of the Society of Archivists, and to those who helped me from the Public Record Office, the Royal Commission on Historical Manuscripts, the Scottish Record Office, and the Business Archives Council. Amongst those who guided me around the general ephemera collections described in Chapter Two, I would like to thank in particular Mr John S. Creasey, Librarian and Information Officer, Institute of Agricultural History and Museum of English Rural Life, University of Reading, Mr Michael Petty, Local Studies Librarian, Cambridgeshire Libraries, Mr Phillip Ward of the Oleander Press, and Mrs Joan Holloway and Professor John Holloway of the Library of Contemporary Cultural Records, English Faculty Library, Cambridge. For assistance on postal history I would like to thank in particular Miss Flint, Librarian, Postal History Collection at Bruce Castle; Mrs J. Ferrugia, Assistant Curator, National Postal Museum; Ms Judith Powell, Librarian, Union of Communication Workers; Mr J.G.S. Scott, Secretary, Postal History Society and many of the various local and national societies listed. For assistance with Valentines and other greetings cards I have to thank particularly Mrs Victoria Moger of the Library at the Museum of London, Mr A.L. Benson, Assistant Curator at the Castle Museum, York; and Miss Jean D. Hamilton, Senior Research Assistant, Department of Prints and Drawings, Victoria and Albert Museum. For general help in finding pictures of domestic appliances I would like to thank especially Mr David Butler, Information Manager at the British Gas Corporation; Mr N.F. Trotman, Librarian of the John Doran Museum, Leicester; Mrs Sarah Carter, Leader, Scientific Information Centre, British Gas Corporation, Watson House; Mr R.G. Hancock, Head of Intelligence and Mr Jack Chapman (formerly of the Electrical Development Association), Head of Publicity at the Electricity Council; Mr Robert Gordon, Curator of the Milne Museum, Tonbridge; and Mr Jim Wood, Curator of the Electricity Council Museum Warehouse in Camberwell. On the topic of visual material more generally I discussed with many people who have knowledge or holdings of relevant materials in the field including Mr Michael Doran, Book Librarian, Courtauld Institute; Mr J.D. Lee, the Librarian, BBC Hulton Picture Library; Ms Louie Boutroy and Mr George Anderson of the Mansell Collection; Mr Hilary and Mrs Mary Evans of the Mary Evans Picture Library; Ms Jane Carmichael of the Photography Department, Imperial War Museum; Mr Andrew Roberts and Mr Richard Light of the Museum

11

Documentation Association. For general help in providing information about the housing field and materials within it I owe a particular debt to Mr W. Pearson, Librarian of the Department of the Environment; Mrs E. Rickman, Assistant Librarian; Mr John Plant, Researcher at the Housing Strategy Office, Greater London Council; Mr George Grimes, Librarian, Self-Help Housing Resource Library, Polytechnic of North London; Mr Alan Gomersall and Mr Tim Owen of the Intelligence Department, Greater London Council; Mrs Mary Orna, Housing Information Officer, London Borough of Camden; Ms Julie Platt, Information Officer at London's Shelter Housing Aid Centre (SHAC). I entered the field of 'community information librarianship' with the help of Ms Judith Bowen of the School of Librarianship at Leeds Polytechnic; Mr Allan Bunch of the Peterborough Reference Library; Mr John Dolan and Ms Pat Coleman of the Longsight Library, Manchester. Others with whom I discussed important aspects of information providing in this field included Mrs Muriel Windsor, Librarian, the Volunteer Centre, Berkhampstead, (and also Secretary of the Aslib Social Science Group). Those who helped me find my way around local resource and information centres included Ms Jane Woddis and Mr Steve Coyne of the Coventry Workshop; and Mr John Allred of the Leeds Trade Union and Community Resource and Information Centre.

All of these individuals and the institutions they represent, and many from all the institutions mentioned in the appendices as well as others too numerous to mention, helped me to put together the information and ideas contained in this book. None of them can however be blamed for any inaccuracies which remain, nor for the opinions set out, which are the sole responsibility of the author. This applies in particular to the British Research and Development Department which funded the work, and the Bodleian Library where it was based. On the other hand, Lesley Bourne, Barbara Kayser and Molly Turpin, who typed the various drafts, must be held responsible for having improved them.

Alan Clinton
London
November 1980

CHAPTER ONE

WHAT IS EPHEMERA?

Those Papers of the Day, the *Ephemerae* of Learning, have Uses often more adequate to the Purposes of common Life than those of more pompous and more durable Volumes.

Samuel Johnson
The Rambler, 145, 6 August 1751

The term 'ephemera' is heard with increasing frequency in many fields. It is used by librarians, archivists, museum curators, collectors and others, in many different senses and reflecting different attitudes, but almost always with reference to printed materials. The aim of this chapter is to set out some of the various approaches and to argue that the disparities that exist cannot be resolved by any sort of semantic consensus, an agreed definition to which all could give at least grudging assent. It will be further argued that in order to resolve the problems of 'difficult' printed materials, it is necessary to go beyond their forms to study their content—to think less in terms of 'ephemera', and more in terms of collections and their subject matter.

The etymology of 'ephemera'
The original Greek word 'ephemeris' means 'diary' or 'calendar' and the word was used in that sense in English until the seventeenth century.(1) This word and its plural form 'ephemerides' (which like its derivatives was used interchangably in the singlar and the plural) had this meaning also, as can be seen from a sermon of John Donne: 'God sees their sins ... and in his Ephemerides—his Journals, he writes them downe'. However, the plural form also began to be used, as indeed it still is, of a branch of astrology, which studies tables of the relative position of heavenly bodies. It was in this sense that Ben Jonson spoke of 'Curses, plagues, piles and pox, by the ephemerides'.

The same word was used in a related sense by Panizzi when he set out the ninety-one rules for the British Museum catalogue of printed books and employed the heading 'Ephemerides' for 'almanacs, calendars

13

of whatever description' and little else.(2)   The word 'ephemera' itself—coming from a neuter plural in Latin but also used in English as if it was feminine singular—had two specific meanings. The first, which has gone out of normal use, refers to fevers which are temporary, or last only a day. The second refers to a type of insect with a very brief life. Thus Samuel Johnson wrote: 'I have three species of Earthworms not known to the Naturalists, have discovered a new Ephemera, and can show four wasps that were taken from their Winter Quarters.'(3)   The term 'ephemera' and the adjective 'ephemeral' were increasingly used in a more general sense. From the mid-nineteenth century they usually had the meaning, short-lived or transitory. Thus Robert Browning:

May I, the ephemeral, ne'er scrutinize
Who made the heaven and earth and all things there.

In one of Auden's finest poems:

. . . the grave
Proves the child ephemeral.

And in another 'the struggle' constitutes:

To-day the expending of powers
On the flat ephemeral pamphlet and the boring meeting.(4)

It has only been in the comparatively recent past that the term 'ephemera' came to be applied to paper in the specific way in which it was conceived for this study. The word was long used of books, as can be seen from the head quotation, but as late as the 1961 edition of *Webster's Third New International Dictionary*, it is only given in relation to insects and in the general sense of 'transient', as also it is in the 1972 edition of *Chambers Twentieth Century Dictionary*. For all that, there has been a growth within the past two or three decades in usage of the term 'ephemera' to apply specifically to paper. This is perhaps in part because of more precise definitions deriving from the development of librarianship, but probably to a greater extent because of its application in the world of collecting. This has been at a time when the use of duplicating, photography and offset lithography have brought about a rapid extension in the quantity of printed material produced, as well as blurring distinctions that could once be confidently made between printed materials and manuscripts.

Before the 1960s there were some references to 'the ephemera of printing' particularly in relation to the collection of John Johnson, then known as 'The Sanctuary of Printing' and housed in the Oxford University Press.(5)   However it does seem that the term 'printed ephemera' and its consistent use for printed sheets of paper must be attributed to John Lewis, and particularly to his excellent illustrated book on the

14

subject, published in 1962.(6) This does seem to be the moment when the term began to be used popularly and widely of printed pieces of paper, and this usage has since come into the language.

Since then, many different definitions of 'ephemera' could be quoted from the world of librarianship, collecting and elsewhere. In practice, it is often separated from minor publications largely by size. 'Ephemera' is also distinguished from 'fugitive material' or 'grey literature' generally on the basis that it is even more difficult to collect, record and find.(7) It is worth looking at three examples from the various discussions by librarians and others on the meaning now assumed by the term 'ephemera'. John Pemberton, whose work provides the starting point for all further discussion of the subject, puts forward the view that 'ephemera' consists of: 'documents which have been produced in connection with a particular event or item of current interest and are not intended to survive the topicality of their message'. Pemberton talks of 'any form of non-manuscript production' but is compelled to include scholarly theses when he looks at items put under the heading of ephemera in certain libraries.(8) This definition of 'ephemera' concentrated on the intentions of those producing it rather than on its use.

The working definition presented before this work began was an attempt to be somewhat more comprehensive: 'A class of printed or near-print documentation which escapes the normal channels of publication, sale and bibliographical control. It covers both publications which are freely available to the general public and others which are intended for a limited and specific circulation only. For librarians, it is in part defined by the fact that it tends to resist conventional treatment in acquisition, arrangement and storage and it may not justify full cataloguing'. This view concentrated less on the form of the material than on its method of treatment. So also does the lengthy definition worked out by the Advisory Committee on Ephemera and Minor Publications which says that ephemera 'does not normally lend itself to standard library procedures of acquisition, recording and storage'. It also speaks more generally: 'Material which comes as a verbal message and is produced by printing or illustrative process but which is not published in standard book or periodical form.'

These carefully worked out characterisations represent the views of individuals who have devoted a great deal of professional care and attention to the subject of printed ephemera, a number of them organised on a representative committee. Nevertheless they are somewhat restrictive in tone and to some degree bound by the concerns of librarianship. If one considers printed ephemera purely from the point of view of its form then it can be located somewhere on a continuum

15

between printed and bound volumes at one end and small scraps of manuscript at the other.

Attitudes to ephemera

In making a more general effort to place ephemeral material at any particular point on this continuum, one is constantly dogged by variations in attitude amongst those who look at and arrange it. To illustrate this, it may perhaps be useful to consider the attitudes of some of those who handle such material. If there is an element of caricature in some of the views it is necessary to indicate, and no individual can be accused of exactly the points of view that are set out, nevertheless it is hoped by portrayal of a number of Weberian 'ideal types' amongst those concerned with this problem to advance towards a method of dealing with it.

a The traditional cataloguer: Readers of *Le petit prince* by Antoine de Saint-Exupery(9) will recall the efforts of the prince to describe his planet to the tiresome and pedantic geographer.

'I also have a flower.'
'We do not record flowers,' said the geographer.
'Why is that? The flower is the most beautiful thing on my planet.'
'We do not record them,' said the geographer, 'because they are ephemeral.'
'What does that mean—'ephemeral'?'

The little prince 'who never in his life had let go of a question, once he had asked it', found it difficult to get an answer from the geographer other than vacuous talk about 'mountains' and 'eternal things'. Eventually however, the definition 'in danger of speedy disappearance' is offered for 'ephemeral'.

Though perhaps this is to create as unkind an archetype as the geographer, there is an attitude in traditional cataloguing which says that material difficult to find and keep need not be recorded. Paper which cannot easily be placed in the well-known categories of author, title, periodical series and so forth can, at least in this archetypal world, be cast out of mind, even if to others it might seem important for its aesthetic merit or for the information it provides. For example, at one time in the 1930s the Bodleian Library threw out a great deal of material that could not be organised according to the rules that then existed, and some decades later welcomed much of it back as part of the John Johnson Collection.(10)

b The traditional archivist: Much of what must be described as 'ephemera' according to any likely definition is kept by archivists, who, because of their view of the 'sanctity' of the arrangements of paper before arriving under their charge, keep printed materials with manuscripts. However, archivists also traditionally make a distinction

16

between 'unique' manuscripts and printed materials, concerning themselves largely with the former. This is despite the problems posed by modern record keeping and changes in printing technology. However the material considered is still a long way along the continuum from the point at which individual items are considered by the 'traditional cataloguer'.

c The museum curator: For a museum curator whose major concern is with objects and artifacts, pieces of printed matter are treated as individual items that need to be described and catagorised without any concern that the description might be larger than the thing described. By the nature of things however, there can be no special consideration of items that are printed and they are usually brought together with artifacts of many kinds from the same location or period, or dealing with the same subject.

d The image librarian: The librarian of photographs, prints and other forms of pictorial representation deals largely in single sheets of paper, sometimes extracted or even torn from larger publications and nearly always including items that can be regarded as printed ephemera. These are never arranged by form but always by content, either from the point of view of the information they provide, or according to aesthetic or iconographic considerations.

e The information librarian: From the point of view of the librarian whose concerns are not at all custodial, information can be gathered from any source, not just written. Ephemeral printed materials will be used heavily, as against other forms of the printed word. They will always be arranged by their content and will normally be within a narrow range of subject matter. Press cuttings, academic reports, encyclopaedias and telephone calls will all have equal status. Much printed material will be ephemeral in a general sense, in that it will be used perhaps once and then discarded.

f The researcher: Like the information librarian the researcher will normally be concerned with the content of the material he studies rather than its form. Even if a particular research topic makes large-scale use of single sheets of printed paper or other material that might be described as 'ephemera', only in special cases will it matter that the material is defined in this way. Again, except in very special cases, the researcher will not look for or find any isolated pieces of ephemera, but will usually use what he does find as part of archival or other such collections.

g The collector: There are collectors whose concern is to bring together pieces of paper for their aesthetic or commercial value or for reasons that cannot easily be ascertained. These pieces of paper can take a particular form—matchboxes, cigarette cards, packaging—or relate to a particular subject—agriculture, pottery, transport. The Ephemera

17

Society, founded in 1975, caters for interests of this sort, from engravings down to certain types of manuscript. It defines its concern as 'printed or handwritten items, produced specifically for short-term use and generally for disposal', emphasising again their 'transient existence'.(11) If only for historical reasons in the organisation of archives and libraries, manuscripts have not been considered in this book, though nearly all the other sorts of items mentioned will require consideration.

Once these separate attitudes are set out, it is possible to see more clearly the limitations of abstractly evolved definitions based on the form of the material being considered. Wherever precisely 'ephemera' is placed on the continuum between books and scraps of paper, organisation of and access to it will only rarely and in special cases be according to its general form. For this reason certain aspects of the general definitions will need to be set aside.

In the first place, there seems little purpose in paying serious attention to degrees of 'ephemerality', which frequently arise from mere abstract consideration of the definition. The Advisory Committee on Ephemera and Minor Publications, for example, has devoted some attention to the difference between bus tickets with a currency of minutes, and share certificates, whose original use can extend for decades. Yet manuscripts, whose originally intended currency can vary just as much, are not traditionally considered from that point of view at all, because the purposes to which they are subsequently put vary so much. Bus tickets would in practice always be placed with other items in a collection on transport, or possibly with other material printed by the same process. There are few purposes for which the length of currency intended by the original producer of an item needs to be taken into consideration after its original use. Its currency at later stages may be even more 'ephemeral' than at first, when the originally proposed length of its life is superseded by the time it has become of concern to those interested in ephemera.

Furthermore, most of the general definitions which have been considered are arrived at by deciding first what to exclude. This negative way of defining 'ephemera' derives from the historically evolved and distinct administrative and professional concerns of librarians, archivists, information scientists and so forth. It is of limited significance for the purposes of collection, access, or organisation. The administrative divisions which have evolved historically in the organisation of information provide the most profound reasons for the existence of the problem which is the subject of this book, well beyond such other factors as the tractability of the material and so forth. It can be no part of any solution to the problem to create a new and special set of vested interests.

18

Having tried to limit consideration of aspects of the matter which may seem important to others, it is necessary to say that somewhere at any rate a real problem exists. There are, after all, ephemera collectors and collections, there is the Ephemera Society, which declared Anno Domini 1980 to be International Ephemera Year. It is for this reason that the following chapter is devoted to considering collections that can generally be described as 'ephemera' or 'printed ephemera'. However, because of the institutional, conceptual and other problems that have been set out there does exist quite beyond this, and on the entire continuum from books to manuscripts, an unsolved problem of large quantities of material over which there is no adequate bibliographical control, which is very difficult to organise and to which there is only limited access. It is the aim of this book to cast some light on what this problem is, and to make some contribution to its solution.

The most rational, if not the easiest, means of doing this has been thought to be to look at collections in various subject fields. Three contrasted fields were chosen: an historical topic, a pictorial subject and a modern social problem. There is no special sanctity in the fields actually chosen, though no doubt they help to colour the general points that have been made in each individual case. Limits which can be said to be quite arbitrary were drawn around each topic; partly to make them manageable, partly also to make particular points in relation to the general concerns of the project. It will become clear that not only do the fields of study vary, but it has also been necessary to consider different sorts of pieces of paper in each case and also very different sets of problems. However, it has been perfectly possible, though approaching the topics essentially *de novo* in each case, to produce with comparative ease lists of collections and other sources which those interested in the respective fields consider more complete than others that exist. This has made it possible, despite all the great disparities in form and content of the subjects under consideration, to go on to propose some general lines along which a solution might be conceived.

The historical topic chosen was postal history. Material in this field, taking Britain alone, largely derives from one source. It is also, even if philately is excluded, of special significance in the world of private collections. This makes it possible to consider a number of particular aspects of private collecting. Also, by considering items sent through the post, the research went beyond the bounds that might have been imposed upon it by purist postal historians. The questions posed by greetings cards, postcards and other such items lead on to more general considerations about organising and finding images.

The pictorial topic chosen was pictures of domestic appliances and

19

purely for reasons of convenience this was limited to items that are powered by gas and electricity. This made it possible to consider the publications and archives of two large public authorities, and a number of particular problems such as commercial secrecy. It was also necessary to look at various approaches to the question of cataloguing images, and at the organisation of catalogue entries which must frequently contain more words than the item being described.

The modern social problem surveyed is housing, which is one of the more difficult fields to deal with from the point of view of bibliographical control and organisation. This is not only because of the diversity of sources that produce literature on housing, national and local, official and unofficial, establishment and anti-establishment. It is also a field with great variation in the form of such publications: print, newsprint, bound, unbound and so forth. Again there is a large public authority at the centre of things, in this case a government department, together with a wide range of other bodies, subordinate to the central authority. There also exist a large number of pressure groups of greater or lesser formality, sometimes working with official bodies and sometimes actively hostile to them. Considering the problems of information in this field led to the appraisal of very diverse types of information provision, including sources beyond those provided on paper. It also led to more general questions of accountability in information gathering and dispersal.

In dealing with these three topics, the subsequent chapters are set out in the following way. For each of the topics considered there is a chapter that outlines how material in the field can be found, and sets out location and organisation of the chief 'collections' in the field, whatever form they take. Each of these chapters is followed by another which sets out some of the more general considerations which arise, from the point of view of collection or access of material in each of the subject fields. (It cannot, of course, be guaranteed that the same considerations would arise had other topics been chosen, but most of the questions considered would apply to many other topics that could have been chosen. Nor indeed can it be claimed that the lists of collections given are complete or without fault. All that can be averred is that more problems in the field are considered than in previous studies known to the author, and that a representative sample at least of the important collections is described.) The second chapter, for reasons already described, deals with ephemera collections in general, and the last chapter contains a summary of the main findings and recommendations for the lines along which the problems that have been considered might be resolved.

20

Some conclusions

The main conclusion of these researches and discussions is that it is both desirable and possible to set up a central and continuing record of information about the material available for the fields that it covers; that it is possible to organise to fill an identifiable lacuna without great difficulty or expense. It is possible to argue, as Pemberton did in 1971, that material could be more efficiently collected in a National Document Library. However this could largely be done if the organisations which presently exist had the resources to do more collecting. It is necessary first however, to take the preliminary step recommended by Pemberton: 'The first requirement is for the establishment of a central register of collections'.(12)

It is essential to set out the problem as plainly as possible. Within the constellation of institutions that presently exist in the organisation of learning in Britain, there are a number of bodies which have evolved historically to perform necessary and distinct functions. The Historical Manuscripts Commission has existed for more than a century to bring together information about manuscript collections and since the 1940s has organised a National Register of Archives to centralise information about such collections. At the opposite end of the continuum of printed paper already outlined is the Bibliographical Services Division of the British Library which sets out the materials—largely books—collected by the Copyright Receipt Office, and records them in the British National Bibliography. In between these two institutions, there exists a number of directories and other information guides, of which the most comprehensive are probably those produced by Aslib.(13) Other guides to libraries, picture collections, pressure groups and so forth could be mentioned. Yet, simply naming institutions is only the beginning of what needs to be done about all the materials that are unrecorded, uncontrolled and impossible to find.

It would certainly be possible, given the resources, to collect more material within the copyright system, and even to do this through the National Documents Library proposed by Pemberton. It would also be possible to produce more and better directories. However, there would still remain the need to collect as much as possible about the basic information at a central source. In the chapters that follow the many forms of this problem will be discussed, but the need for a unified approach will be argued throughout. The final chapter will set out on this basis the need for and the functions of a proposed National Register of Collections.

NOTES TO CHAPTER ONE

1 This account draws heavily on the *Oxford English Dictionary* and most of the quotations are taken from there unless otherwise

stated.   There is also a discussion on definition in Rickards, M *This is ephemera.   Collecting printed throwaways* Newton Abbot, 1977, 7-8, from a somewhat different point of view.

2   *Catalogue of Printed Books in the British Museum I* (1841) ix.

3   In *The Rambler*, 82, December 29 1750.

4   Browning, R *Aristophanes' apology* 1875, 127; Auden, W H 'Lullaby' (1932) in *Collected poems* Faber, 1976, 131, 'Spain 1937' in *The English Auden*, edited by E Mendelson, 1977, 212.

5   Jackson, H *'Signature'* November, 1935.   See also Bodleian Library Oxford *The John Johnson Collection.   Catalogue of an exhibition* edited by M L Turner, Oxford, 1971, 11.

6   Lewis, J N *Printed ephemera: the changing use of type and letter forms in English and American printing* 1962.   The word is also used in the article by Lewis in *Motif* 1961 and of course in his *Collecting printed ephemera.   A background to social habits and social history to eating and drinking to travel and heritage* 1976.   It is interesting to notice that J K Melling's delightful little volume *Discovering theatre ephemera* 1974, includes 'paper, cardboard, cloth, wool, metal and even stone'.

7   Sturges, R P *Local publications as a problem in bibliographical control* unpublished paper 1979, discusses some of the distinctions. See also the 1980 BL R & D Report of R P Sturges and D Dixon.

8   Pemberton, J *The national provision of printed ephemera in the social sciences* University of Warwick, 1971, 6, 11.

9   In the Pan Piccolo edition of 1974, translated by Katherine Woods, 54.

10   See the 'Introduction' by M L Turner to *The John Johnson collection.   Catalogue of an exhibition* Oxford, 1971, 12-13.

11   *The Ephemerist* November 1975; *Evening News* November 10th 1975.

12   Pemberton, 47, 43.

13   Aslib Directory Volume I *Information sources in science, technology and commerce*, edited by E M Codlin 1977; Volume 2 *Information sources in Medicine, the Social Sciences and the Humanities*, edited by B J Wilson.

CHAPTER TWO

GENERAL EPHEMERA COLLECTIONS

It is difficult to describe it except by saying that it is everything which
would ordinarily go into the waste paper basket that is not actually a
book. Another way of describing it is to say that we gather everything
which a museum or library would not ordinarily accept if it were offered
as a gift . . . Collected in this wide area they render us open to the
banter of the world.

John Johnson on his Collection(1)

One of the main conclusions of the chapters that follow is that in order
to resolve the problems of dealing with printed ephemera, it is necessary
to go beyond the category itself. Various definitions and uses of the
term have been discussed in the first chapter to show the difficulties
that arise from its use. In each of the subject fields considered in subsequent chapters the clear dividing line between ephemeral printed
materials and other objects of collection and research breaks down.
There are however some collections which can be called 'ephemera
collections' or are so described, and it is to these that this chapter is
devoted.

The world of printing and its history

Any account of general ephemera collections must begin with the name
of John Johnson (1882-1956) who was Printer to the University of
Oxford from 1925 to 1946. His collection began in part because of the
restrictive acquisition policies of librarians, it developed through an
interest in printing and found its final resting place in the Bodleian
Library in 1968.(2) Its organisation is under a very general but comprehensive list of headings, and in most cases no effort is made to list
individual items. The collection aims to cover every kind of non-book
printed item down to letter heads and invitation cards; though in
practice it also includes manuscripts, postal history, postcards and
much else that is not 'pure ephemera'. Although Johnson took a special
interest in printing history, he ultimately went a long way beyond it.

The files of jobbing printers have in a number of cases provided information both for those interested in the development of printing itself and the details of the phenomena covered by the subject matter. Perhaps the earliest example of this was when the National Library of Wales began to collect such material in 1909 from the firm of Thomas which printed in the *Tivyside Advertiser* in Cardigan. This material provided a wide range of information about local social, religious, sporting and other activities though not on any systematic basis.(3) Many examples of the work of two printers, John Soulby father and son of Ulversten, were brought together along with related items such as the products of their competitors. These are now in Barrow-in-Furness Library, and the Reading Institute for Agricultural History where they can be used to illustrate the development of printing from 1796 to 1827.(4) Similar information can be gathered from the sample books of a jobbing printer of Ware from 1908 to 1920 now at the Hertford-shire Record Office. Another collection from the printing firm of John Proctor of Hartlepool and his successors was collected by a local historian called Robert Wood, and is now to be found in the Hartlepool museum, where it is being carefully arranged in a system set out in Appendix One.(5)

It was collections of this kind, starting from an interest in the development of printing, but then moving on to consider more general information, that led after 1960 to the development of the study of 'ephemera' as a separate category. Although John Johnson had taken the initiatives in this direction, access to his collection was restricted before it was moved into the Bodleian in 1968. It was probably John Lewis more than any other individual who developed an interest in 'ephemera' as a category, and as seen in Chapter One, he was almost certainly the first person to use it in print in the sense in which it is now commonly employed. Starting from an interest in typography and printing history, Lewis, who was denied entry to Johnson's Collection during Johnson's life, went on to see the more general interest of non-book printed materials. His book *Printed ephemera*, which first came out in 1962 contained no less than 713 illustrations, many in colour, not simply to illustrate the development of typefaces, but also many aspects of social and economic life.(6) Since that time Michael Twyman has used such material to illustrate in a scholarly way the history of printing more generally, and Louis James has presented by-ways of nineteenth century social history by similar means. The material from letter heads has also been used in an imaginative way to illustrate shop fronts in the era before photography.(7) The study and illustration of packaging has also developed, both for its aesthetic and social interest.(8) This soon leads on into the world of collecting, from cigarette cards, match box labels to pot lids and beer labels.(9) Posters and playing cards are only two other collectors items that could be mentioned with their own special world and, of course, their own prices. Some of the general problems posed by the existence of private collectors of materials of this sort will be discussed in Chapter Four.

Private collectors and the Ephemera Society
The spread of the usage of the term 'ephemera' amongst archivists and librarians in the late 1960s was both a result of the publication of John Lewis and of the growth of interest in collecting. At the beginning of 1969, an exhibition of such material from private collections was held at Foyle's in Charing Cross Road in London, and later in the same year articles began to appear in scholarly publications.(10) This interest amongst the organisers of knowledge was extended by the wider publicity given to the exhibition of the John Johnson Collection in 1971 accompanied by an excellent catalogue. 1971 also saw John Pemberton's report on *The national provision of ephemera in the Social Sciences*, and the various discussions that followed on this. Since that time the special category of ephemera has been referred to by archivists, antiquarian booksellers and many others, but the optimism of Pemberton that there might be some resolution at least for currently produced material, has diminished in recent, more difficult years.(11)

The private collectors of the varieties of materials that have been mentioned not only inhabited their own private worlds, but also had more general concerns. It was to cater for them that the Ephemera Society was set up in 1975 by Mr Maurice Rickards. This Society has organised sales, lectures and other activities and has to an increasing extent won the interest of company archivists, librarians, academics and others. It declared 1980 to be International Ephemera Year and ran various exhibitions, sales and so forth in connection with it.(12)

Ephemera collections in libraries and museums
It has been developments and discussions such as these that have brought about a concern amongst librarians, archivists and museum curators with the preservation of printed throwaways in a way that was not common twenty or thirty years ago. Numerous examples could be mentioned, of which the following are typical. At the National Library of Scotland, efforts are being made to bring together ephemeral material produced in elections throughout Scotland. Much similar material is to be found in the Modern Records Centre at the University of Warwick. The Centre has a great deal of ephemeral material relating to political activity, industrial relations and other such topics.(13) Closer to the world of the collecters and also to the Ephemera Society are the various items in the Department of Prints and Maps, Guildhall Library in the City of London, including book plates, playbills, playing

cards and a number of other items of which more details are given in Appendix One, Item 10.(14) Similar material is brought together in the Ephemera Collection at the London Museum, though this is smaller and on the whole more recent. Ephemeral printed material of a general sort is to be found in the Tolson Memorial Museum in Huddersfield, and in the Country Life Archive of the National Museum of Antiquities of Scotland.(15)

It is the development of such collections as these which has brought a renewed interest in some of the materials to be found in national collections. A number of the general headings in the British Library Reference Division can reveal nineteenth century material of the ephemeral printed variety, single sheets, cards, lithographical pictures and so forth. It usually takes some effort to extract what is to be found there, and the recording of individual items can be quite inaccurate. Diligent searching under such headings as Ephemeredes and Collections can reveal a great deal of interest to the world of typography, popular art and so forth. Under Ephemeredes are almanacks and printed diaries, including those from temperance movements, political and religious organisations and many more. Under Collections are the Joseph Ames Collection with several thousand title papers and collections of alphabets. Other well known collections include those of Bagford, Banks (including prospectuses) and Fillenham (including Christmas cards and posters). They also include engravings, broadsides, newspaper cuttings, religious tracts, handbills and materials covering various towns. Perhaps surprisingly in view of Panizzi's rules, some parcels of calenders are also to be found under this heading at the shelf mark 1899 f f 1 in six rather dusty parcels for the period 1899 to 1914, with as many as thirty different examples of ephemeral popular art. In the British Library depository at Woolwich there is also a row of shelves containing material not otherwise catalogued, including bus timetables, postcards and much else. Other material of which outsiders and new employees are only vaguely aware is also to be found in any large library. The Bodleian Library now has the advantage that nearly all such material can in principle be subsumed in the John Johnson Collection, though there are of course separate collections of broadsides and other single sheets from long before the days of John Johnson.

Subject and local collections
There are two other sorts of artificial general ephemera collections that should be mentioned. The first exist as part of collections in various relevant fields. Thus, for example, the Institute of Agricultural History at the University of Reading contains much material of this kind, some examples of which have already been mentioned. Appendix Five Item Seven gives more detail. The Shoe Museum in Northampton

includes a similar specialist collection of material. Many other specialist collections could be mentioned like the great range of material in the Theatre Museum presently located in the Victoria and Albert Museum, the materials at the Wimbledon Lawn Tennis Museum, the Bryant and May collection of matches and labels in the Science Museum and the materials (including audio-visual) in the Archive of the Centre for English Cultural Tradition and Language at the University of Sheffield. The field of transport would provide many other such examples, perhaps headed by the materials kept at the British Rail Museum in York, the London Transport Museum in Covent Garden, London and the Beaulieu Motor Museum. The Hudson Collection in the Science Museum, London has 60,000 railway tickets and Mr Gordon Fairchild has a private collection of similar size.(16) To cover such collections in any detail would be, however, to go well beyond the scope of this book.

One other sort of ephemera collecting is that which has been in co-ordination with traditional local history collections and more contemporary 'history from below' research. Thus for example, the Museum at Appletongate, Newark in Nottinghamshire tries to bring together locally produced materials, as does the County Record Office in Ipswich, Suffolk. Such material is also available in Newcastle-on-Tyne Local History Library. The more systematic study of what is known as 'street literature' has come from the bringing together of such materials in the past.(17) In particular the materials brought together in the Cambridgeshire Collection at the Central Library Cambridge since the mid-nineteenth century, allow serious use of ephemeral literature for social history. Interesting local studies are already possible as a result of the Central Library Collection together with what is contained in the Cambridge Papers at the University Library, the County Folk Museum, and the Library of Contemporary Culture Records in the English Faculty Library.(18) Similar work has been made possible by looking at the Museum and Record Offices in Chepstow, Gwent.(19) This in turn is only one part of the rapidly expanding and multifarious activities to be found in the study of local history. The proposals of the recent Committee under the Chairmanship of Lord Blake which dealt with these matters will no doubt stimulate improved education, access to archives and further forms of work in the field.(20) There is already a good deal of evidence of efforts to approach the available materials in a more imaginative and systematic way.(21)

Conclusion

It would be possible to continue this survey almost indefinitely. One might, for example, consider the general and particular collections to be found in the United States and elsewhere beyond this island. However, even within the entirely artificial limits that remain, it has been possible to show that there are many non-archival collectors in numerous subject fields and local areas whose existence is hardly recorded or known. To separate the 'ephemera collections' from the many forms of paper which are considered in the rest of this book may be valuable for some conceptual purposes. However, the best way to treat the particular problem of printed ephemera, to encourage its collection and to improve access to it, is to look at it from the point of view of its use and relevance. Enough differences already exist because of the dividing lines between the current organisers of knowledge without thinking of ways of dealing differently with all of the forms of knowledge which have been considered in this study. That is why the central section of this book aims to seek out and find collections of materials relevant to particular fields of research. In this way it is hoped to get beyond the conceptional problems to see how the real difficulties can be resolved in practice.

NOTES TO CHAPTER TWO

1 Quoted in Bodleian Library Oxford *The John Johnson Collection. Catalogue of an exhibition* edited by M L Turner, Oxford 1971, 11.

2 Besides the introduction to the catalogue, see *Times Literary Supplement* 3 October, 1968: Laquer, T 'The John Johnson Collection in Oxford' *History Workshop*, 4 1977; Ridler, V 'Desiderata for the sanctuary of printing' *Signature* 5 1937. See also the first entry in Appendix One, page 97 below.

3 For details see Ballinger, J *Gleanings from a printer's file* Aberystwyth, 1928.

4 Twyman, M and Rollison, W *John Soulby, printer, Ulversten* Reading, 1966.

5 Middleton, H 'The Hartlepool find' *The Ephemerist*, January 1979 on the collection in general and Wood, R *Victorian delights* 1967 for examples arranged under topics. Lewis, J *Collecting printed ephemera* 1976 has a commentary and many examples from this collection.

6 Lewis, J N 'In pursuit of ephemera' *Motif* 7 Summer 1961, *Printed ephemera. The changing use of type and letterforms in English and American printing* Ipswich, 1962. Lewis has also produced *Collecting printed ephemera. A background to the social habits and social history to eating and drinking to travel and heritage and just for fun* 1976, which is somewhat less systematic but also of interest.

7 Twyman, M *Printing 1770-1970. An illustrated history of its development and uses in England* 1970, containing 880 illustrations, many from John Johnson; James, Louis *Print and the people 1819-1851* 1976 is largely derived from it. See also Vaisey, D and Turner, M L *Oxford shops and shopping* Oxford, 1972.

8 Humbert, C *Label design* 1972; Davis, Alec *Package and print* 1973; Turner, M and Vaisey, D *Art for commerce* 1973.

9 London Cigarette Card Company, *British cigarette card issues 1888-1919* 1973 and *1920-1940* 1974; Rendell, J *Match box labels* Newton Abbot, 1968; Ball, A *The price guide to pot lids* 1977; Osborn, K and Pipe, B *Beer Labels* 1979. For a slightly different approach see Melling, J K *Discovering theatre ephemera* 1974.

10 See *The Guardian* January 11 and *The Times* January 12, 1968. Storey, R 'Printed ephemera in 1968' *Business Archives* June 30, 1969; Hepworth, P 'Manuscripts and non-book materials in libraries' *Archives* IX October, 1969.

11 For later discussions see Stockham, P 'Design registration marks as an aid to bibliography 1842-1900' *Antiquarian* IV September 1977, drawing attention to printed ephemera in Registration Books in the Public Record Office. See also Storey, R *Printed ephemera* Business Archives Council Broadsheet 7 1977, and Storey, R and Madden, L *Primary sources for Victorian studies. A guide to the location and use of unpublished materials* Chichester, 1977, 64.

12 Rickards, M *This is ephemera. Collecting printed throwaways* Newton Abbot, 1978 gives some of the philosophy and attitudes behind the Society and *The Ephemerist* which has appeared since November 1975 outlines its activities. An example of Mr Rickards' talent for publicity, as well as an account of his private collection is to be found in *Evening Standard* March 19, 1980, 23 in an article by McGill, A 'History in the waste bin'.

13 Details are to be found in Storey, R and Druker, J *Guide to the Modern Record Centre, University of Warwick Library* 1977 and in the quarterly *Information Bulletin* produced by the Centre.

14 See Guildhall Library *Guide to the London Collections* 1978.

15 National Museum of Antiquities of Scotland *The County Life Archive–A Short Guide* 1975.

16 Fairchild, G 'Tickets for all seasons' *The Ephemerist* January 1979. Mr Fairchild is the moving spirit of a Transport Ticket Society, which has produced since 1969 a regular list of *Ticket companies and titles* The Ephemera Society Exhibition *Going places* used such material and a publication by Edmund Swinglehurst entitled *Collecting travel and transport ephemera* is promised as this book goes to press.

17 Early studies in the field are Shephard, L *The history of street literature* 1973 and Collison, R *The story of street literature forerunner of the popular press* 1973.

18 For an excellent example, including an account of the material see Ward, Philip *Cambridge street literature* Cambridge, 1978.

19 Waters, Ivor *Chepstow street literature and ephemera* Chepstow, 1979.

20 *Report of the Committee to Review Local History* Standing Conference for Local History, 1979.

21 See for example Petty, M J 'The resources of nostalgia: local studies libraries' *Library review* Spring 1979.

CHAPTER THREE

POSTAL HISTORY

There are . . . many reasons why collecting postal history is so popular today, why it is so absorbing and satisfying. It rightly qualifies as the 'number one' for personal pleasure and attraction.

A.J. Branson
Introducing postal history 1978, p4.

Of all the hobbies in the world, collecting old picture postcards is the easiest to master, without having to wade through a mountain of reference books in search of knowledge.

W. Duval and V. Monahan
Collecting postcards in colour 1894-1914
Poole, 1978, p28.

Postal history was chosen as a field with a large historical sweep and a continuing output of considerable scope, much of which can be traced to one source. It is also a field for private collectors but is covered inadequately in reference books and centralised lists. It inevitably presents its own particular problem of scope and definition but makes it possible to consider some general questions of the arrangement of archives and private collections.

Definitions
For the purposes of this study it was thought best to exclude philately. Adhesive postage stamps are well enough catered for in commercial catalogues, and are comparatively easy to arrange by date and price. In Britain, the firms of Stanley Gibbon and Robson Lowe have long been dominant in the field, and major collections are generally arranged according to the catalogues they produce.(1) This applies for example to the British Library Philatelic Collection, which is currently being considered with a view to a comprehensive, computerised catalogue. This may well set the pattern for such operations in the future.

If postage stamps are to be excluded, then what of postmarks and handstamps? These are clearly printing under certain definitions, and have been the object of the most devoted and detailed study at least since the late nineteenth century by those describing themselves as postal historians.(2) There are some in the field who regard 'the study of handstamps stuck on letters' as being the first part of any serious definition of 'postal history'. However, others have more recently tried to extend it. 'Postal markings are only one facet of such a study, on a level with such documents as Post Office Acts, broadside, posters etc.' This led on to a more comprehensive definition formulated by Professor West when he was at the Philatelic Unit of the University of Sussex. This was based on a definition worked out by the British Postal History Society in discussion with the Federation Internationale de Philatelie: 'Postal History is the study of letter sheets, covers, cards and related items in reference to written communications transmitted by recognised means. The words 'related items' includes postal markings, postal rates, decrees and documents pertaining to postal service, censorship of mail, military mail, field post, siege mail and V-mail, POW and concentration camp mail, ship letters, postal propaganda and other materials'.(3) This might seem comprehensive enough though it clearly straddles the dividing line between printed and manuscript items. If it can be expanded to include all materials relevant to a study of the history of the postal system in Britain, then it is possible to set out some particular and general sources.(4)

Major national collections
A great deal, though by no means all, of what is relevant in this field is housed in the Post Office in St Martins-Le-Grand in London. Though formerly a Department of State and now a 'designated authority' the Post Office has always kept its own records apart from the Public Record Office, and has resisted spasmodic efforts to terminate this arrangement. The material is largely archival in character, including minute books, letter books, files, together with various guides, sets of printed reports and so forth. There is also a small section of 'artificial' collections by place, and some according to broad subject matter such as Staff, Maps and Telegrams. Other relevant materials include volumes of newspaper cuttings and indexes of relevant parliamentary papers. Some more recent sections are not on open access. More detail is given in Appendix Two.

There are a number of other relevant national collections. The largest and best of these is Bruce Castle in Tottenham, North London, once the home of Rowland Hill—who campaigned for the penny post—and now containing, inter alia, a large collection of material on postal history, broadly conceived. The original core of the material was the private collection of H. V. Morten, who was telephone manager in

Nottingham at the end of his career. Morten's collection of paper and artifacts was bought after his death by the Union of Post Office Workers in 1923. Since 1928 it has been kept in Bruce Castle and run by the local authority. There is a small museum and a collection of papers. A good deal has been added to the collection since it first went to Bruce Castle. Thus for example it now contains some of the diaries of Rowland Hill and a collection of stamps and postmarks donated by H. G. Fletcher in 1968. The items are divided separately into box files 1700-1840, pamphlets after 1800, smaller pamphlets, books, engravings, objects and posters, according to a scheme outlined in detail in Appendix Two.(5)

The National Postal Museum in the London Chief Office largely concentrates on collections of strictly philatelic interest, though it contains some other items. The same applies to the Royal Philatelic Collection which is held in Buckingham Palace(6), and to the library of the National Philatelic Society at the National Liberal Club in London. It may also apply to the Library of the Royal Philatelic Society, which is unfortunately not open to outsiders. The new Bath Postal Museum only began to acquire material at the same time as this survey.

Amongst other national institutions the British Library contains a great deal of non-book material on the postal services. This is partly in the Philatelic Collection and in the Reference Division spread through many parts of the library, a few examples of which are given in Appendix Two. The John Johnson Collection in the Bodleian Library contains the F. A. Bellamy collection of postage stamps and Postal History for which there is a manuscript catalogue. The National Maritime Museum has a small but important collection.(7) There are postal history collections in at least three other museums. The Castle Museum, Norwich, has an active policy of bringing together such material, and the Science Museum in London has the important Penn-Gaskell Collection on air mail. The Tolson Memorial Museum in Huddersfield has another small collection from Frank Buckley covering Yorkshire postal history 1744 to 1850. There is also a small collection in the library of the Victoria and Albert Museum. It is worth mentioning the collections of the two major trade unions in the Post Office. The Post Office Engineering Union has sent most of its historical records to the Modern Records Centre at the University of Warwick, though it does not contain a great deal on the postal system as such. The Union of Post Office Workers, which has been actively collecting material since its foundation in 1920, has this arranged by its own numerical sequence, and is currently being photographed to save space. Some sections of this are of general relevance for postal history.

Specialist and local collections

Although most archival collections of any sort like the Public Record Office or the House of Lords Record Office can be made to yield relevant material, specific collections relevant to postal history are to be found in a number of public archives. Some of these can be identified through the National Register of Archives and some by means of the various clubs and societies in the field. The NRA, for example, allows the location (at NRA 14455) of the collection of Samuel Graveson in the Hereford County Record Office. Graveson was one of the pioneers of postal history and a founder of the Postal History Society. He sold most of his collection, but what remained was mostly of local interest, and he donated it to his local Record Office in the 1940s. This can be studied in association with a number of individual items from other collections. Details are given in Appendix Two. Four other County Record Offices are also covered there. The Surrey and Suffolk Offices are given as examples of collections containing very limited amounts of relevant material, at least accessible for the purposes of this study. The Staffordshire and Derbyshire offices both contain material referred to in the NRA, and the former contains little else that can be found. In Derbyshire, however, there are some other materials, and these are described in Appendix Two.

One important collection to which it is possible to gain access through the clubs and societies network is the material in the Leeds Public Library from the Leeds Philatelic Society, which has a significance well beyond philately. Most aspects of the postal history of Yorkshire can be covered from this, and there are also relevant books and periodicals, some of them very rare. The City of Manchester Archives Department has some material in the Charles Roeder Collection and an indexing system that makes it possible to retrieve more from elsewhere. Items of local interest are to be found in the archives in the Halifax Central Library, and in the Local Collection in the Uxbridge Library. At least three local libraries have at one time collected books of postal history interest. They are the Holborn Central Library in Kingsway in the London Borough of Camden which has a fair number of local histories, the Reference Library at the Arndale Centre, Poole, Dorset, and the Central Library, Duke Street, Chelmsford in Essex. Unfortunately Chelmsford and Holborn have now abandoned this specialism.

Private collectors and their clubs and societies

In going beyond the public domain in this field to private collections, one is immediately faced with some special problems. It is a field almost entirely occupied by non-professional collectors. A great deal of material is held in private hands and much of it is very valuable. Some of the problems this presents in strained relations between

34

archivists and postal historian are discussed in the next chapter. A little of this same hostility to 'outsiders' was experienced by the present writer, though it must be said that a great deal of courteous advice was also offered. As a result of discussions with the Postal History Society, and the various other bodies in the field which are listed in the appendix, it became clear that it would be quite impossible to produce any list of collections held privately.

The Secretary of one local society told me that his members 'would obviously not wish to advertise to the criminal fraternity the whereabouts of valuable accumulations of postal material in private hands'. With regard to what is said to be a collection brought together by another local Society I was informed as follows: 'It is not available for examination or viewing by non-members for security reasons, but we would try to answer specific requests for information—always remembering that we are an amateur organisation and dependent on voluntary workers . . .'.

This is a typical attitude. The general Postal History Society and the Society of Postal Historians to which people well known in the field are elected, both construct lists from time to time of the 'interests' of their members, and these turn up with the files of their publications in the British Library. The lists provide another means of entry into the materials, though it is difficult to see them being used by those for whom postal history is of more marginal interest, say as part of a more general local study. Only one of all the officials of the various societies consulted expressed himself in favour of a register of private collections, though even he suggested it would have to be kept secretly, with access only to trusted specialists in the field.

For all of these reasons, it is not possible to set out a list of private collections. One local secretary tells me that he has 'found from experience that persons of similar interests or engaged in similar lines of research will usually very rapidly become aware of others so engaged by means of a very efficient "bush telegraph" '. The problem with this is that though it may be true of the enthusiasts, there is no reason why it should apply to outsiders who see postal history in a more general context. It is for this reason that the appended list includes the main societies in the field and their officials in 1979. It should be pointed out that most enthusiasts belong to more than one society so that it is comparatively easy to get into the network. The local societies naturally vary a great deal and it is not possible within the limitations of the concerns of this book to track down every last one. However, it can be taken that the appended list includes the strongest and most active, for England at any rate.(8) To make the project manageable, if for no other reason, foreign specialists have been excluded, as also have such bodies as the Letter Box Study Group.

Another means of entry into this field of private collections is through the main dealers in the field, all of whom issue catalogues giving details on individual items, though rarity rather than historical value is thought to be their greatest interest. The catalogues of Harmers and Robson Lowe are to be found in the British Library and those of Stanley Gibbon are also widely available.

Greeting cards and picture postcards
Though not strictly within the province of postal history, it is worth while devoting some attention to items sent in the post, including greeting cards and postcards. This is because such items loom large in a number of more general collections, and they are important for the problems of arrangement and cataloguing discussed in later chapters.

Valentine greetings were sent in the days of Chaucer and Shakespear.(9) Greeting cards were hand painted during the eighteenth century and began to be sent in large numbers with improvements in printing technology and the introduction of the penny post in 1840. In 1850, 102,000 were sent in Britain, in 1857, 897,000 and in 1883 (the highest figure) 2,768,000. The figures then fell dramatically to under half a million in the 1890s, though the fashion had by then taken on in the United States and Germany.(10) By this time, the sending of Christmas cards had become more common, and the sending of picture postcards in Britain can be dated from 1895. The beginnings of the collecting of Christmas cards can be dated quite precisely to the 1890s, as also can the first picture postcard collections.

By far the largest collection of Valentine cards from the period of their greatest popularity in Britain was made by Jonathon King of Essex Road Road, Islington, London. These were meticulously pasted into volumes with such headings as Humorous, Topical, Boxed and Sentimental. In the 1870s King's collection was written up in the local press and twenty years later was well known internationally. In 1911 King offered his collection, which was then said to contain 250 volumes, to the British Museum. The Museum authorities said they would only accept a part of it, and King refused this condition. The result was that it was left to rot after King's death in 1912. Some parts went to London Museum and a little ended up in the John Johnson Collection, but most of what remained went to the Hallmark Collection in Kansas City, United States.(11)

The Museum of London now has about 30 boxes, albums and separate groups of Valentine cards from King's collection comprising approximately 1900 cards together with various accompanying cuttings, letters and so forth. The British Library Reference Division, as far as can be ascertained from the catalogue, has a few Valentines of which examples are listed in Appendix Three. Other significant collections are to be found in the Department of Prints and Drawings of the Victoria and Albert Museum, in the Castle Museum, York and in the John Johnson Collection in the Bodelian Library Oxford. There are smaller collections in the St Bride's Painting Library and in Shell-Mex House, London, WC2. Details of these collections are to be found in Appendix Three. This has only become a field for private collections and dealers within the last decade or so, but they have already pushed up the price of nineteenth century Valentines to a minimum of £5 or so and a maximum of £100 or more.(12) Although the Christmas card developed somewhat later, it became more general and widespread. It was deliberately invented in 1846 by Sir Henry Cole, first director of the South Kensington Museum, and has become commonplace since. Collections began as long ago as the 1890s. However, perhaps because of their inferior aesthetic merit, fewer examples are to be found in libraries and museums and private collectors have only shown a comparatively limited interest.(13)

Picture postcards are collectors items of considerable importance. The sending of picture postcards first began in Austria in 1869 and spread throughout Europe in the 1890s. Only from 1902 was it possible to send postcards in Britain which were entirely covered by the picture on one side. In 1899, 88 million cards were sent in Germany, 14 million in Belgium and 8 million in France. Already collecting had begun and by 1914 it was a veritable craze. In that year the extraordinary total of 926.5 million postcards were sent in Britain, not all necessarily with pictures.(14) In 1933 the term 'cartophily' was coined by C. L. Bagnall to describe the collection of all forms of small pictures including trade cards and cigarette cards. This became a world of its own, with its special conventions and values. The word 'deliology' (originally 'deltiology') was coined in 1933 by Randall Rhodes to describe specific collecting of picture postcards, usually of topographical interest.(15) A number of such collections have already been mentioned, but material relating to Scotland is to be found in the National Library of Scotland, and a large collection of over 3000 cards on aeronautical subjects with the Penn-Gaskell Aeronautical Collection in the Science Museum deals with aircraft, airships of various sorts, personalities in the field and so forth. Mr R.A. Storey, Archivist of the Modern Records Centre at the University of Warwick, has a private postcard collection which is naturally better organised and accessible than most. Entitled 'Words and Machines' it has separate headings for Aviation(A), General (G), Horsedrawn Transport(H), Industry(I), Motor Transport(M), Shipping(S) and Tranways(T). Various methods of cataloguing by subject matter are discussed in Chapter Six.

NOTES TO CHAPTER THREE

1 Stanley Gibbon Ltd *Postage stamps catalogue* is divided into separate volumes for the British Commonwealth (plus Ireland and South Africa), Europe and Colonies, America, Africa and Asia. Each of these appear annually. Robson Lowe produces *An Encyclopedia of British Empire postage stamps* 1952 etc which is more detailed. There is also a *Catalogue of the Philatelic Library of the Earl of Cranford* 1911, plus supplements on what is now in the British Library. See also Negus, J 'A brief guide to the sources of philatelic information' in *Philately* VII 1959, 102-3, 116, 121.

2 The study which began as a sub-branch of philately perhaps with Daniels, J H *A history of British postmarks* 1898 has flourished since the setting up of the Postal History Society in 1935, which now has numerous offshoots and regional equivalents.

3 Willocks, R M *The postal history of Great Britain and Ireland. A summarised catalogue to 1840* 1972: quotation from the blurb of the publisher who is also the author. The other quotations are from Cornelius, D B *Devon and Cornwall. A postal survey 1500-1791* 1973 piii and West, J C 'The study of postal history' *Business archives* 36 1972 36.

4 Bibliographies in the field include Strange, A M *A list of books on the postal history, postmarks and adhesive postage and revenue stamps of Great Britain* (Great Britain Philatelic Society 1964). John Noyce produced three other useful compilations dating 1968 and 1969 which were published as supplements to *Postal history news*, and entitled 'Local British postal history. A select bibliography', 'Posts and post offices in Britain' and 'The campaign for cheaper postage in Britain in the nineteenth century'. By far the best book on the subject is Robinson, H *The Post Office. A history* Princeton, 1948, though this is rather thin on the recent period, a defect to some extent supplemented by the same author's *Britain's Post Office* 1953. Haldane, A R *Three centuries of Scottish posts* Edinburgh, 1971, is also worth mentioning. On collecting, besides the source in the head quotation there is Prince Dimitry Kandaouroff *Collecting postal history* 1973, which is profusely illustrated.

5 Flint, E A *A guide to the Postal History Collection, Bruce Castle Museum, London N17* 1974 is the most recent account though there is more detail in Rock, C H 'The Postal History Collection at Bruce Castle Tottenham', *The museums journal* October 1934 and his *Guide to the collection illustrating the history of the Post Office* Tottenham Museum, 1938. See also London Borough of Haringey *Bruce Castle Museum. A guide to the buildings and collections* c 1978.

6 Wilson, J *The Royal Philatelic Collection* 1952.

7 Staff, F *The Transatlantic Mail* 1956 gives detail of the main material covered.

8 The British Philatelic Federation *Yearbook* of which the 1979 volume was used contains the fullest list of postal history societies and much else besides.

9 Staff, F *The Valentine and its origins* 1969, gives the fullest account. See also Webb Lee, Ruth *A history of Valentines* 1953, and Calder-Marshall, A 'Valentines' in Hadfield, John (ed) *The Saturday book* 1966.

10 Figures calculated by the Post Office for Jonathon King in the collection in the Museum of London, in the Album entitled 'The artistic lithograph'.

11 This story can be gathered from the cuttings, letters etc in the same album, though this gives the *Daily Mail* of February 11, 1898 saying there were 1000 volumes in the collection. The sequel was told by Mrs Victoria Morger in a lecture given at the Musuem of London on February 8, 1979.

12 Discussions of the market now appear in the main newspapers every February—for two recent examples see Hiller, B 'Valentines for everyone' *The Times* February 11, 1977 and Hadden, C 'Dearest second-hand love' *Sunday Times* February 10, 1980.

13 Ettlinger, L D and Holloway, R G *Compliments of the season* 1947, Bundy, G *The history of the Christmas card* 1954, and Seddon, L 'Season's greetings' *The Ephemerist* November 1979. An article in *The Standard* for Christmas 1894 by G White on 'Christmas cards and their chief designs' proposes that they should be collected by the British Museum so that 'in a few decades they would appear "quaint" and "curious" and finally be appreciated as very interesting *ephemera* of a very interesting period of English art-production'.

14 Staff, F *The picture postcard and its origins* 1966; Casline, R *The pictures in the post. The story of the picture postcard* (2nd edition 1971 by J R Busclich); Kyron, A *L'age d'or de la carte postale* Paris 1966; Report of the Postmaster General on the Post Office for 1913-14 (Cd 7573) 2.

15 Scully, P 'Joys of cartophily' in Hadfield, John (ed) *The Saturday book* 32 1972, 172; Klamkin, M *Picture postcards* Newton Abbot, 1964, 8.

CHAPTER FOUR

ARCHIVISTS, COLLECTORS AND HISTORIANS

In the arrangement of an archival collection the interests of historical
research should receive only secondary consideration.
> S. Muller, J.A. Feith and R. Fruin
> *Manual for the arrangement and description of archives*
> New York, 1940 p55.

In a field where co-operation is needed it is pointless to ignore the fact
that our interests are opposed. If we recognise this, we can see how
best to reconcile them . . . we feel that a letter goes into an archive
and is absolutely dead.
> R.M. Willcocks
> 'The archivist and postal history' *Postal history* 173
> March-April 1972, p178.

It cannot be denied that real differences of interest exist between those
who look after research materials and many of those who wish to use
them. Collections held in private hands, whether archival or 'artificial',
and collections held by those professionally concerned with their
preservation also present difficulties from the point of view of access
and use, which do lead to the conflicts frankly acknowledged by Mr
Willcocks. It is hoped in this chapter to set out some of the differences
that exist with a view to proposing some ways in which compromises
can be reached.

Attitudes of private collectors
With a few conspicuously important exceptions, most of the collections
which have been listed for the study of postal history either began, or
still are, in private hands. One of those active in the field expressed the
view to me that 90% of the relevant material remains in private hands.
This is simply an impression, and it is of limited importance for those
outside the freemasonry of the collecting world itself, who will find
access much easier through public institutions.

Now there is a problem in the field of private collections, most especially in the particular field covered in this study, that must be squarely faced. It has been said that 'all collecting . . . extinguishes the moral instinct. The object finally possesses the possessor'. It is well known that in collecting there develops a 'cash nexus' which in many fields 'has drowned the heavenly ecstacies of religious fervour, of chivalrous enthusiasm, of philistine sentimentalism, in the icy waters of egotistical calculation'.(1) The nature and consequences of this can be seen very clearly in the field of postal history, even leaving aside philately. There is a market where many individual items, including 'ephemera' according to the strictest definition, regularly change hands for many hundreds of pounds. Thus during 1972-3, the firm of Robson Lowe sold 3334 items of 'postal history' at £159,739 an average price of £47.90. In 1977-8 the same firm sold 1713 items for £149,162, almost doubling the average price to £91.16 for each item. A catalogue from the firm of Harmers for a sale held on 21 February, 1979, shows that the cheapest of the 595 lots was expected to fetch £10, and one envelope was thought likely to be sold at between £1000 and £1,500.(2) This is perhaps the only field where valuable scholarly articles can be written from material that changes hands at such prices.(3)

Although it is possible for outsiders to console themselves with references to the cynic who 'knows the price of everything and the value of nothing',(4) there are nevertheless some real problems. Not only are there difficulties in gaining access to private collections, leading to compromises of the sort suggested in the last chapter. Even the collections in public hands have to be guarded with the utmost care. The losses from one of the major national collections in the 1960s are well known and it is now more adequately protected by a former policeman. I have seen elsewhere collections which are not in practice open to public view at all, with active steps taken to discourage knowledge of their existence. The person responsible for at least one of the collections listed was not at all keen to appear in a 'national register', though the collection is well known to those in the field and appears in a number of reference books. At another collection, I was scrutinised to check my identity, and higher authority had to be consulted to check an alleged irregularity in my driving licence.

Attitudes of archivists
As a result of this security problem, real hostility has at times manifested itself. Almost thirty years ago, long before prices had reached anything like their present exhalted level, one archivist described what was happening as a result of postal historians getting to private papers before they did: 'How many archivists have not seen the results of an investigation (sic) made by a philatelist? It is the exception rather

41

than the rule to find a collection of correspondence public or private of a date when valuable philatelic items are likely to be found, which has not undergone the attention of these collectors'. The writer (who in his seething rage has not bothered to distinguish between philately and postal history) went on to warn of the breaking up of 'archive groups', the removal of individual items, and the discarding of many others. Thus there was a serious danger that important documents 'may be converted into lampshades or toy drums'.(5)

Examples have been quoted of collections like the Codrington Correspondence between the West Indies and Britain being broken up and sold for their value as collectors' items of postal history and not preserved for their obvious interest to historians of colonialism and international trade. Warnings have been issued by archivists in the sternest tone: 'Owners of family papers and those to whom correspondence of any kind has been entrusted are warned against advertisements or direct requests for the purchase of covers bearing early postal marks. The argument is often advanced that the removal of the cover does not impair the value of the letter. This however is rarely true, for the addressed and postmarked cover is part of the letter paper itself, while in many cases the cover constitutes the only evidence of the name and address of the recipient of the letter. Correspondence can be invaluable for many subjects, but, if it is deprived of such vital evidence, it ceases to be of value, either to the historian or from the monetary point of view.' A letter appeared in *The Times* on May 23, 1961 from Mr Brian Redwood, Secretary of the British Records Association, along similar lines.(6)

In an age when monetary inflation is so prevalent that it is nearly always thought preferable to hold wealth in any form but money, it is perhaps inevitable that the 'cash nexus' will throw its shadow over collections in many fields. Entry into private collections will be difficult, and some means of overcoming this problem have been suggested. As for collections in public hands, it is clear that fairly vigorous forms of security involving large scale expenditure on manpower is a necessary part of granting access to valuable materials contained therein. It is however essential that such material should be publicly owned and available as well as properly recorded. Without some effort to do this it will simply become impossible to gain access to important aspects of human knowledge.

There is however, one other serious problem about collections of material in public hands, including many considered in the last chapter and this arises from the nature of their custody and organisation. As the discussion on archives quoted at the very beginning of this chapter makes clear, archivists do not start out from the interests of the consumer of their product. This point is made even more forcibly in another standard account, defining a document as an archive if it 'was drawn up or used in the course of an administrative or executive transaction (whether public or private) of which itself formed a part; and subsequently preserved in their own custody for their own information and by persons responsible for that transaction and their legitimate successors'. One result of this definition is that the duties of an archivist are set out as follows: 'They are primary and secondary. In the first place he has to take all precautions for the safeguarding of his Archives and for their custody, which is the safeguarding of their essential qualities. *Subject to the discharge of these duties* he has in the second place to provide to the best of his ability for the needs of historians and other research workers. But *the position of primary and secondary must not be reversed*.'(7)

Now these fundamental principles, which it must be said are not usually understood by those who use archival collections, are of considerable importance for research of the sort being considered here. Local record offices begin as arms of local government, dedicated to preserving and then organising the documents of this activity. Researchers are not always aware that the primary concern of the Historical Manuscripts Commission is to make lists, rather than to provide a direct means of access to private papers and public archives. The National Register of Archives and its subject index are only a partial outgrowth of this. Having said that, it should be pointed out that at least some of the references in this book to collections of interest in postal history have come from the NRA. At least two of these references could not have been found any other way. It seems virtually certain, however, that there are many other such collections which could not be discovered by this means.

The need for subject indexing
Archivists have particular duties to perform in the preservation of records and there is no reason why registers should include more information than the name implies. However, the conception of simply listing documents from the working of institutions does create difficulties. For example, it can mean that the criteria for the selection of papers for preservation may be correct from an archival point of view—as part of the development of institutions—but less helpful for the purposes to which the documents are actually put.(8) Once archives get to any age, their use for institutional purposes tends to diminish. Historical studies have gone to some trouble to break out of institutional straitjackets, and record offices increasingly contain collections which are 'artificial' in the archival sense. For this reason it is important to emphasise that without the subject indexes and similar research tools

43

that exist, it would not have been possible to do much of the work of this project. Furthermore, this applies at a level still one removed from research itself.

In the case of at least one record office, subject indexing has been abandoned altogether in recent years in favour of more complete, though by no means more comprehensive, listings. Though often cases could be quoted where the trend is the other way, there is an attitude among some archivists that to produce 'vertical' listings, subject indexes and so forth, is to abandon their 'real' work for what should be done by the researchers themselves. However, for the researcher also *Vitae summa brevis spem nos vetat incohare longam*, life is too short to allow us to enter into far-reaching hopes.(9) A large proportion of the entries in Appendix Two and a number in Appendix Three could not have been found at all without the existence of various forms of subject index well within the 'secondary' functions of the custodians of the material in question. It would be possible in the postal history field to cooperate with practitioners and amateurs to produce indices in the local record offices which could be used for a national or overall survey. There are other ways in which access could be granted to this material when the will exists to go beyond its initial institutional order.(10) There has also been a trend recently for particular subject fields to look after the materials in which they themselves are interested. Some such examples have already been quoted in Chapter Two on general ephemera collections, including the Institute of Agricultural History at Reading and the Shoe Collection in Northampton. A number of agencies devoted to listing collections of materials in specific fields are given in Appendix Four. These are quoted as examples of the sorts of organisations which are developing to fill a clear need. Others of the same sort could be mentioned in the fields of literature and elsewhere, with the character of the listing varying by subject. They fill a need to those in their respective fields, but are not necessarily well known to those on their fringes.

A plea for mutual understanding
There is one final point that needs to be made particularly with reference to material of the sort that is being considered in this study. Without dreaming of a Utopia where all knowledge is recorded in every possible way, it is nevertheless possible to consider modifying a certain attitude of mind that is nurtured by the institutional boundaries in which it grows. Librarians, like archivists, are trained to begin with lists organised not by likely use, but by alphabetical sequence, by form and so on. In the more rarified higher reaches of the profession the arrangement of vast masses of material, even books, in ways in which

they cannot be used except by other librarians is thought of as an end in itself. However, there are encouraging signs of efforts to break out of the 'tyranny of the list'. Users of the more recent sections of the British Library catalogue and also of the British National Bibliography are certainly aware of more means of access to books than in the days of Pannizzi and his ninety-one rules. The development of community information librarianship, discussed in a later chapter, also shows a healthy trend towards being concerned with organising knowledge itself rather than the forms in which this knowledge is recorded.(11)

As well as the 'tyranny of the list', librarians have also been known to suffer from 'the tyranny of the catalogue'. This assumes that all forms of arranging paper must be subject to the same strict rules that can apply to books. If they were to look over their shoulders into the museums they would discover a very different attitude. Within the John Johnson Collection in the Bodleian Library, there are a good number of boxes of Valentine cards. Because they are now within a library, those responsible for its preservation would not dream of listing the individual items contained in these boxes. However, when precisely the same material ends up in a museum, the attitude is quite different. Museum curators are quite used to describing items that do not have authors or titles. Thus in the Print Room Catalogue at the Victoria and Albert Museum one Valentine is described as 'expanding flowers containing two hearts (1825)' and another as 'A Ship of War, the hull of which opens to show a sailor visited by Cupid c 1840-51'. The Castle Museum, York, contains an entry in its accession list at 538/46 as follows: 'A valentine, with a beautiful picture in the middle of a huge bunch of different coloured flowers. In the centre sits a boy and a girl being crowned with a crown of roses by two cherubs and at her feet is a cherub offering her a rose. It is called Rose Beauty. Also written on the card is a verse

This lovely queen of the bowers
Is like thee in every part,
As it reigns over the flowers
So dost thou over my heart.'

Such detail might perhaps be regarded as excessive, but opens the possibilities of entry to the collection other than by the simple category of 'Valentine'.

There is within the various professions mentioned an increasing awareness of the need to provide better means of entry into collections of material. Some efforts have been made, for instance, to work out classification systems for particular forms of archives.(12) In Chapter Six there is a description of the activities of the Museum Documentation Association. There have been efforts to produce a more comprehensive and also computer based method of record in the archive world, though

45

perhaps they have not gone so far as the MDA.(13) It can only be hoped that the mutual incomprehension of collectors and archivists and others can be overcome in the production, hopefully in co-operation, of lists and other tools that allow entry to the various forms of collections.

It must be emphasised that seen from any one point within the world of learning and its organisation, the problems posed in this chapter may appear quite different from how they have been viewed here. In searching out the collections in the field of postal history, the relations between the collectors, archivists, researchers, museum curators and others have at times been characterised by real hostility, but more often by misconceptions. Researchers are not always aware of what archivists regard as of primary importance, and those within the professions that organise learning can sometimes be directed towards a set of activities which seem highly parochial to outsiders. Catagories like that of 'ephemera' itself, built up within institutional walls or in the special world of collecting, are of limited value in the 'real world' of research, even in the form described in the previous chapter. In looking at other forms of collections, it will soon become clear that often categories and jurisdictions evaporate also.

NOTES TO CHAPTER FOUR

1 Fowles, John *The Magus* Triad/Panther edition, 1977, 178; Marx, Karl and Engels, Frederick *Manifesto of the Communist Party* 1847 in *Collected Works* Volume 6 1976, 487.

2 Robson Lowe Ltd *Annual Review for 1972-3, Annual Review for 1977-8*, Harmers of London *Catalogue of postal history . . . to be sold by public auction . . . on . . . February 21, 1979* 1979.

3 An example which is of interest beyond the very narrow concerns within the specialism is a piece by the Secretary of the Postal History Society, based on privately held material commercially acquired by Scott, J G S 'Sir Andrew Agnew and the Sunday Posts' *Postal history* 173 March-April 1972.

4 Wilde, Oscar *Lady Windermere's fan* Act III.

5 Sergeant, E H 'The archivist, the postal historian and the philatelist: co-operation or collision?' *Bulletin* of the Society of Local Archivists December 1951, 20-21.

6 *Archives* II 9 1953, 46-7, V 26 1961, 107; Business Archives Council *Quarterly bulletin* 12 October 1961, 7-8.

7 Jenkinson, H *A manual of archive administration* 1937, 2nd edition 11, 15 (with original emphasis). But see pp85-6, below, for more recent views.

8 For an interesting account of valuable statistical material for social history disappearing for these reasons see Whiteside, N *New uses for*

public records RAD Occasional Papers 3 1975. The destruction of the early census returns is a more well-known example.

9   Horace, *Odes* I, iv.

10   Storey, R A 'Indexing archives' in *The indexer* V 1967 gives some excellent advice on arrangements to allow greater access.

11   I am most grateful to John Allred of the School of Librarianship at Leeds Polytechnic for developing this point for me. See also Kemp, D A *The nature of knowledge* 1976 and Chapter Seven below.

12   Philips, D 'A classification system for agricultural engineering archives' *Business archives* 41 January 1976.

13   See McCall, F *Prospec manual* PRO, c 1975 and Roper, M *Prospec-SA: pilot project. The development of PROSPEC for wider use in providing guides to record offices. Final report* BL R & D, September 1978.

CHAPTER FIVE

FINDING PICTURES OF DOMESTIC APPLIANCES

Now, around 1920, mechanisation involves the domestic sphere. For the first time it takes possession of the house or whatever in the house is susceptible to mechanisation.

> S. Giedion *Mechanisation takes command.*
> *A contribution to anonymous history*
> New York, 1948, p42.

The universal use of externally powered domestic tools has become so much part of day to day life that it is easy to forget both its relative novelty and the powerful impact it has exercised on the private world of almost every person. Over thirty years ago, when Giedon wrote his stimulating book about the impact of the changing development and design of household appliances on domestic and social organisation, he included many illustrations. Nevertheless he found it necessary to complain, at least for the United States, of: 'an amazing historical blindness that has prevented the preservation of important historical documents, of models, of manufacturers' records, catalogues, advertising leaflets and so on'.(1) Although it is perhaps possible to say that the more recent position in Britain is not as bad as that, there are gaps that could be identified and possibly filled after the creation of a central record.

Forms of material

Before considering in detail the places to go in Britain to find pictures of domestic appliances, something should be said of the form taken by the relevant materials. In looking into the archival holdings of two major nationalised industries, some private companies and at museums and picture libraries, it has been necessary to look beyond the individual pieces of paper which were considered under the category of postal history.

One source containing large amounts of relevant pictures are the catalogues produced for advertising and information since the eighteenth

48

century. If such materials cannot be described as 'ephemera' according to the generally agreed use of the term, they can be said to be 'ephemeral' in almost every other sense—little noticed, seldom systematically arranged, and rarely used for the invaluable pictorial information they contain. It is true that for some time there has been an interest in older forms of trade cards.(2) It is also the case that sales catalogues have long been used by scholars to trace individual books, and generally to describe the book trade.(3) Sales catalogues have also been used more recently to trace the details of landed property and housing, and this will be made easier by local historians and archivists who have been retaining them. Thus the Local History Library in the London Borough of Barnet keeps sales catalgoues from the mid-nineteenth century, though they are not separately catalogued, and the Surrey Record office in Kingston-upon-Thames keeps a separate file of 'sales particulars', including detailed descriptions of various sorts of property in the county.(4) It has only been in the quite recent past, however, that efforts have been made to collect and make available the information contained in trade catalogues. An exhibition in the Manchester Polytechnic Library in May 1978 has stimulated interest in the subject and such materials in the Victoria and Albert Museum, the Science Museum and the Science Reference Library are being looked at and arranged more carefully.(5) This has been part and parcel of an effort to look more seriously at business records. House journals and a number of other such items of entirely passing interest do not seem to be collected even by the most diligent of copyright librarians. However, the Business Archives Council is now giving advice to a wide range of commercial undertakings about what materials to keep and how to keep them.(6) It is to be hoped that as a result a great deal more advertising and similar matter will be available in the future.

History and general sources

Domestic appliances entered the homes of the rich in the late nineteenth century, but the more widespread use of externally powered machines coincided with the disappearance of domestic service after the First World War. Though removing one part of the household hierarchy, their use tended to reinforce some other parts of it. Thus if anything the new appliances have in the past increased the sexual division of labour, since it has been in the interests of those selling them to emphasise their domestic rather than social application, and to strengthen the institution of the nucleated household.(7) For reasons which are no doubt related, there has been remarkably little change in the design of powered domestic appliances, often little altered from whatever manually operated machine they have replaced, or else with a stark functionalism that renders them almost invisible.

In looking at the development of the appliances themselves, it is possible to see many gaps between invention and use. Gas was first used for lighting in the 1840s, generally adopted by 1870, and rapidly replaced by electricity with the production of a workable light bulb in 1911. Gas cookers existed as early as 1812 but were not widely sold before the 1890s, nor generally adopted until the 1920s. By then the electric cookers that had existed since the 1880s were being marketed, though with rather less success. In the same period before 1914 a 'hygenic revolution' brought about a new and careful delineation for bathrooms as a separate feature of domestic architecture. Special machines for heating water and space date from the 1880s, and their adoption can be dated from the turn of the century, in the same period of gramaphones and radio sets. It was the spread of these forms of domestic entertainment in the 1920s and 30s that increased demand for domestic connection to the electricity supply system. Hand irons go back at least to the early nineteenth century, though electric irons began to be sold in the 1890s. Vacuum cleaners were first sold in 1901, and practical electric kettles in the 1920s. Electric washing machines were marketed in the USA in 1907 and in Britain about ten years later. Domestic refrigerators powered by electricity were sold in the USA in 1912 and in Britain in 1921. Gas refrigerators came after 1933. The widespread use of domestic washing machines and refrigerators in Britain can only be dated from the 1950s when they came in with the ubiquitous television.(8) Appliances in both fields were made by a wide range of private manufacturers and used power supplied by a large but diminishing group of private and public undertakings which were eventually brought under central public control in the 1940s.

For purposes of this study, appliances powered by means other than gas or electricity are largely omitted. This arbitrary dividing off of the subject matter of the study nevertheless leaves a very wide range of sources and forms of material to be considered. Besides the archive and information services of two major nationalised industries, it has also been necessary to look at a wide range of materials emanating from manufacturers and retailers, and at what has been collected outside the industries themselves in museums, picture libraries and elsewhere. Some of the many forms taken by the materials to be found there have already been considered.

A number of general sources can be used to find pictures of domestic appliances, and details of how they are arranged are given in Appendix Five. The domestic appliances gallery at the national Science Museum has hundreds of separate artifacts within the range of items already set out, and beyond it. There is a systematic policy of photographing these items, which cover all aspects of the field and are looked after by people with a wide knowledge and contacts with others who have

50

similar collections. The photograph and slides collection of around 500 items is not enormous but it covers the main types of items in the field. The department also possesses some ephemeral material including a good number of trade catalogues. Materials connected with electric lighting and gas production are to be found in other departments of the Science Museum. Another general source for such material is the slide library at the Design Centre, which contains relevant items in a number of forms. A third general source is the Science Reference Library, where efforts are being made to bring together trade catalogues on a systematic basis.

Pictures of domestic appliances are also to be found in a number of museums, libraries and picture collections. Thus the Country Life Archive of the National Museum of Antiquities of Scotland in Edinburgh has a systematic policy of collecting pictures of interest and as a result contains many useful items. There are relevant items also in the Welsh Folk Museum in Cardiff. The Institute of Agricultural History and Museum of English Rural Life at the University of Reading has a larger collection of photographic material and business archives within its own field, including a limited amount that is relevant to the particular concerns here. There are many record offices and other depositories that could also be mentioned, and details of materials in the Scottish Record Office are given in Appendix Five as an example of what might exist in many other such places. The same could probably be said of the John Johnson Collection in the Bodleian Library, and of the pictures to be found in the BBC Hulton Picture Library, the Mary Evans Picture Library and the Mansell Collection. The particular parts of these collections where material relevant to this study is to be found is outlined in Appendix Five, and there is a general discussion about the problem involved in organising images in the next chapter.

It is possible to use all of these sources to find individual pictures of domestic appliances. However, to trace the changes in design and technology in a more systematic way, it is necessary to turn to the industries themselves. Thus although the gas industry has no statutory obligation to preserve its records, it has made considerable efforts to do so. Similar steps are also being taken within the electricity industry.

The gas industry
The Institution of Gas Engineers has set up a Panel for the History of the Industry, which includes representatives of its various parts, and has contacts on every level. The Panel aims to encourage the preservation and proper care of artifacts and archives of the industry and to record them through a computerised retrieval system based on the Information Retrieval Group of the Museums Association (IRGMA) and entitled PHILIS (after the Panel for the History of the Industry Location and

Information System). Local area bodies of the Gas Corporation are encouraged to deposit artifacts at museums and archives at public record offices. Details are then kept at a central source, and it will eventually be possible to retrieve them through the PHILIS system.(9) Lists in the files of the Panel are at this point generally rather fragmentary. For instance an 'Inventory from Croyden Works Old Records' ends with the information that it includes: 'Envelopes and albums containing many old photographs'. Nevertheless the work of the Panel will no doubt help Trevor Williams who is writing the history of the industry. It has already helped to produce at least one quite systematic account of the development of gas appliances, with many pictures, as well as serious work which has been undertaken in the East Midlands on the local history of the industry.(10) Lists of people interested in various aspects of the development of the industry have been compiled by the Panel, and these provide access to relatively inaccessible collections and other sources of information.

Partly as a result of these efforts, a number of museums now exist within the gas industry. The North Thames Gas Board is considering the creation of a museum at one of its London sites. Greater progress has been made by the East Midlands Gas Board which opened the John Doran Museum in 1977. This contains a great deal of documentary material as well as artifacts. With a little help from the Regional Board's advertising department the Museum is well organised and items are accessible, though the total number of pictures of domestic appliances is not great. All items are individually recorded in a numbered inventory which it is hoped will eventually go onto the PHILIS data base.(11) The inventory is currently being put onto cards in more detail and arranged by subject and manufacturer, which will increase its usefulness.

By far the most comprehensive collection of pictures of gas domestic appliances is to be found at Watson House in Peterborough Road, Fulham in South West London. This is the British Gas research station which deals with the domestic utilisation of gas. Details on all appliances to which approval has been given over the last fifty years are arranged according to a system explained in Appendix Five. Although this is much the most comprehensive collection of its kind, for reasons of commercial confidentiality not all the information it contains is necessarily available to outside enquiry.(12)

The electricity industry
Few electrical appliances predate 1900, and their spread was slow before 1930. As late as 1918 only 6% of homes in Britain were connected with electricity, and even in 1938 the figure was only 65%, with the great majority of appliances still used for lighting.(13) The
52

romance of this early stage of the development of the industry was noticed by Sir John Betjeman in the *Baker Street Station Buffet:*

Early Electric! With what radiant hope
Man formed this many-branched electrolier,
Twisted the flex around the iron rope
And let the dazzling vacuum globes hang clear,
And then with hearts the rich contrivance filled
Of copper, beaten by the Bromsgrove Guild.(14)

The somewhat slow and difficult efforts of the electrical industry to establish itself in the domestic consumer market resulted in the publication of numerous books about the wonders of electricity, and a wide range of advertising materials.(15) In particular these came from two organisations: the Electrical Development Association, set up in 1919 and in 1965 merged with the publicity department of the Electricity Council, and the Electrical Association for Women, founded in 1924 and still publishing relevant material.(16) Although the EAW apparently does not keep systematic records of its former activities, its publications together with those of Dame Caroline Haslett, its founder and leading light for most of its existence, contain a great deal of relevant illustrations.(17) The records of the EDA, largely consisting of advertising material for electrical appliances, provide the largest source of illustrative material in the field found during the course of this research. Details are given in Appendix Five.

Like its competitors in gas, the electricity industry also set up in 1973 a widely representative committee to organise what is known as the National Archive for Electrical Science and Technology. The aim of this body is: 'to locate original material relating to all aspects of the history of the electrical and electronic science and technology. The material will if necessary be sorted, recorded and deposited in a suitable regional repository or retained by NAEST. NAEST will establish a centralised record of the location, content and accessibility of relevant material already available in libraries, record offices, firms and private collections'.(18) Some of the items relevant for this study which have been collected in the archive are set out in Appendix Five.

The electricity industry has also got a number of repositories which include artifacts and associated materials. The most important of these is the Milne Museum which was set up in 1971 and opened in 1975 in the Tonbridge District Council Electricity Generating Station. This includes a wide range of household appliances which are well organised and interestingly displayed. There is a collection of books and also a large mount of archival material which the part-time curator of the museum has not yet been able to arrange systematically.(19) The Electricity Council Museum Warehouse set up in 1975 in Penrose Street, Camberwell, London SE17, concentrates more on the production side of the industry and is not normally open to the public. The warehouse nevertheless has some appliances to show as well as albums, scrapbooks and other relevant materials.(20) There is also a collection of Electrical Antiquities, run by the East Midlands Electricity Board and moved to Nottingham in 1979.

The private entrepreneur

There is one other general source for materials in this field besides the large public institutions and their various agencies on which attention has so far been concentrated. This is the private manufacturers and retailers of the appliances themselves.(21) The useful role of the Business Archives Council in helping to preserve and record such material has already been mentioned. However, it must be said that these materials are not usually easily accessible to outsiders, particularly when they are making general enquiries of the sort in this project. There are examples of the use of some of the resources of private firms in this field(22) though it is very clear that, particularly on the retail side, systematic records of any kind are very difficult to come by.(23) There is however an archivist at the John Lewis partnership who controls some relevant material. On the producers' side, Ferranti Limited have well catalogued material in their archives for the appliances they have sold, and Hotpoint and Hoover are prepared to respond to individual enquiries. Belling has taken some pride in its archival records in the past, but seems nowadays to be less open to outside enquiries.(24) This is a field where the private collector of 'antiques' can and does provide information and pictures, as well as prices and methods of exchange.(25)

Further research among individual firms would no doubt reveal more material, but there would be increasing problems of accessibility, and there would be little purpose in pursuing them from the point of view of the narrow concerns of the current project. Besides the problem of availability, there is also the question of extracting the relevant information from what is discovered and it is to this that the next chapter is devoted.

NOTES TO CHAPTER FIVE

1   Giedion pv. The illustrations used in the book are mostly advertising materials, mainly from company archives. Some use was made however of the Bella C Landauer Collection of ephemera at the New York Historical Society.

2   Heal, A *London tradesmen's cards of the XVIII century* 1925; Calvert, H R *Scientific trade cards in the Science Museum Collection* HMSO, 1971; Baily, J L 'Trade literature: its nature, significance and treatment' *Business archives* December 31, 1969.

54

3 In 1915 the British Museum published a *List of catalogues of English book sales 1676-1900 now in the British Museum*. This was extended in the international listings of Frits Lugt beginning with *Répertoire des catalogues de ventes publiques* The Hague, 1938. Examples of more recent listings in the field are Feather, J P *Book prospectuses before 1801 in the John Johnson Collection* Oxford, 1976, and Munby, A N L and Coral, L *British book sale catalogues 1676-1800* 1977.

4 For examples of the use of such material primarily for landed property see Gillies, A J 'Surrey Estate Plans' *Bulletin of the Society of University Cartographers* VII August 1972 and Hillier, R 'Auction catalogues and notices: their value to the local historian' *Local historian* XIII 1978 131-9.

5 Manchester Polytechnic Library. *An exhibition. Historical trade catalogues. May 1978* 1978.

6 For accounts of how this was carried out, see Wadsworth, J E 'Businessmen, bankers and the Business Archives Council' *Business archives* 36 June 1972; Orbell, J 'The Business Records Advisory Service of the Business Archives Council' *Ibid* 44 November 1978. Details of advice are given in Business Archives Council. *The management and control of business records* 1966.

7 For convincing arguments on these points see Forty, A 'Electrical appliances 1900-60' in *Design 1900-1960* (ed) Faulkner, T Newcastle-upon-Tyne, 1976, 104-6 and Cowan, Ruth S 'The industrial revolution in the home: household technology and social change in the twentieth century', *Technology and culture* 17 1966.

8 For general summaries on this see Giedion p512f; de Hann, D *Antique household gadgets and powered appliances c 1860 to 1930* Poole, 1977; and Brooke, S *Hearth and home. A short history of domestic equipment* 1973. On the sources of power see 'A history of gas appliances' *AGA monthly* September 1976 and the Electricity Council *Electricity supply in Great Britain. A chronology* 1977. On particular types of domestic appliances see Swenarton, M 'Having a bath. English domestic bathrooms 1890-1914' in *Leisure in the twentieth century* Design Council, 1977, 94; Wright, L *Home fires burning. The history of domestic heating and cooking* 1964; Norwak, M *Kitchen antiques* 1975 including a most useful list of 'Kitchens, houses and museums to visit' p131. *Design*, journal of the Council for Industrial Design, contains numerous relevant articles—see for example Stafford, J 'Gas cooker' in the issue of May 1954 dealing with changes in design from the 30s to the 50s, Howe, J 'Domestic equipment. A survey of modern powered appliances for the home' July 1957, 'Fifteen years of cooker design' July 1965. These sources can be supplemented from Coulson, A J *A bibliography of design in Britain 1851-1970* Design Council, 1979.

9 For more detail see Butler, D R 'PHILIS—making history useful as well as diverting' *Gas world* March 1979, 154 and 'The preservation of the historical records of the British gas industry' private publication of the British Gas Corporation, 1979.

10 Crawford Sugg, P *Using gas, yesterday and tomorrow* IGE, 1979; Roberts, D E *The Leicester gas undertaking 1821-1921* Leicester, 1978 and *The Sheffield gas undertaking 1818-1949* Leicester, 1979.

11 Trotman, N F and Nixon, E C A *A numerical inventory of the EMGAS historical collection housed at the John Doran Museum Aylestone Road Leicester* 1979.

12 There is a useful survey of another source 'Fifty years of corporate gas advertising' in *Gas engineering and management* May 19, 1969 by C L Maunder and A Sheppardson, which has many different illustrations though unfortunately does not give the sources.

13 Hannah, L *Electricity before nationalisation. A study of the development of the electricity supply industry in Britain to 1948* 1979, 186; Corley, T A B *Domestic electrical appliances* 1966, 19. Hennessey, R A S *The electric revolution* Newcastle-upon-Tyne, 1971, discusses the slow spread of electricity at some length almost entirely from the point of view of the producers.

14 Betjeman, Sir John 'The Metropolitan railway Baker Street Station buffet' (1954) in *Collected poems* 1970, 212.

15 For examples see White, A G *The all-electric age*1922 containing many illustrations and Philips, R R *The servantless house* 1920.

16 Hannah *op cit* p77f and Messenger, R *The doors of opportunity. A biography of Dame Caroline Haslett* 1967, 50f.

17 In particular Haslett, C *The electrical handbook for women*, which went through various editions in 1934, 1936 and 1945 until the sixth edition in 1956 now entitled *The EAW electrical handbook*. See also Haslett, C *Household electricity* 1939, revised as Electrical Association for Women *Household electricity* 1960.

18 From the explanatory leaflet on its activities.

19 For a general account see Arnott-Job, Jane 'Granny's attic and what you might find there' *Electric living* Spring 1979.

20 Hood, W H *Catalogue. Electricity Council museum warehouse* nd.

21 Jeffreys, J B *Retail trading in Britain 1850-1950* Cambridge, 1954, 405-13 traces *inter alia*, the decline of the individual suppliers and the growth of the multiples. (Books about the companies active in the field say very little about the design and development of appliances —for example Whyte, A G *Fifty years of electrical progress. The story of GEC* 1930; Lee, N and Stubbs, P *The History of Dorman Smith 1878-1972* 1972; Bloom, J *It's no sin to make a profit* 1971; Jones, R and Marriott, O *Anatomy of a merger* 1970, on GEC, AEI and English Electric.)

22 Wood, M and N *Home in the twenties and thirties* 1978 makes good use of some company materials, along with magazines and periodicals. Jackson, A A *Semi-detached London. Suburban development life and transport 1900-39* 1973 makes interesting use of brochures and postcards, though not for domestic appliances.

23 For some efforts to rectify this see Poole, L 'British Business Archives—1 The John Lewis Partnership' *Business archives* 37 December 1972, Godfrey, H 'The archives of J Sainsbury's Ltd' *Ibid* 44 November 1978.

24 Jukes, G *The story of Belling 1912-1962* Enfield, 1963 is better than most such volumes. Some leaflets and trade catalogues of the firm are in the British Library, though none relevant for this study.

25 See Curtis, T *Kitchen equipment* 1977 in the series *Antiques and their values* published by Lyle Publications of Galashiels, Selkirkshire, Scotland, and Jo Marshall *Kitchenware* 1976 in the series *Collecting for tomorrow* which contains a good range of excellent pictures and their sources, as well as a bibliography.

CHAPTER SIX

THE ORGANISATION OF IMAGES

Now, for an absurdly small sum, we may become familiar not only
with every famous locality in the world, but also with almost every man
of note in Europe . . . we . . . have . . . looked . . . through a three-inch
lens at every single pomp and vanity of this wicked but beautiful world.

Once a week 1 June 1861

Marx reproached philosophy for only trying to understand the world
rather than trying to change it. Photographers . . . suggest the vanity
of even trying to understand the world, and instead they propose we
collect it.

Susan Sontag *On Photography*
1979 Pelican edition p82.

Dramatic improvements in the techniques for reproducing images have
not simply expanded the sum of knowledge of the world, and granted
sensory access to what was once utterly outside almost every experience.
They have also, as Susan Sontag acutely understands, made possible
the accumulation of images and, one might go on to say, their systematic
organisation. The family albums, the postcard collections, the magazine
archives have been built into libraries of images. At the same time
pictures from the highest to the lowest aesthetic merit and information
content can be brought together in one place, or access can be granted
to them to a much greater extent than ever before. If our sensibilities
become jaded by images of the starving, the beautiful and the interesting,
then we can at least consider retaining the pictures for other purposes
and other information they may contain.

These reflections have been induced by the problems encountered
in looking for the particular images described in the previous chapter,
and by considering how the materials investigated are organised from
the point of view of other possible reasons for looking at them. Many
of the institutions described have their own comprehensive methods of
arranging ephemeral printed materials and so forth under their charge.

58

However, they often do it according to their own particular history or their present concerns, and not in such a way as to make very easy the extraction of pictorial information, most especially when it does not constitute the first thing likely to be noticed about an individual picture.

Forms of arrangement in picture libraries
The fundamental difficulty in retrieving information from pictures derives from the traditional way in which the great picture collections have been organised by form rather than by content. Where other methods are used they often reside simply in the heads of individuals and, like Topsy, 'just grow' without definite plan or reason, simply from what was originally there and the use to which they have been put. In the art history world there can be no doubt that in any forms of organisation beyond the names of artists, schools and methods of reproduction it could be said by the individuals who work out the systems that:

Players and the painted stage were all my love
And not the things that they were emblems of.(1)
In such great art libraries as the Courtauld Institute, it is much easier to retrieve the items it contains by names of artists and schools than by what the pictures contain. Nor do the concerns of iconography 'with the subject matter and meaning of works of art rather than their form'(2) really help a great deal. The most well-known and exhaustively comprehensive system of granting access to every aspect of the art output has been set up in the Netherlands. Entitled the DIALS Index, and based on the so-called Iconclass system, it is of value for finding representatives of 'Mercy' or 'the Holy Ghost', but not much good for oil lamps or the changing fashions in seventeenth century dress.(3)

However, there are indications in the art history world and beyond of a realisation of the need to go further than 'analysing, signs symbols and meanings'; to cater for the increased use of visual materials by disciplines other than art history by means of subject indexes and the use of computers to coordinate efforts.(4) One person who has worked in the intermediate field of setting up a computer catalogue including medieval illuminated manuscripts and early printed books set out the problem very well.(5) He pointed out how pictorial 'documents are essentially "lost" if users do not know they exist or cannot locate the desired materials'. Catalogues however usually 'classify their holdings according to art historical criteria: artistic medium, artist and provenance'. The challenge for curators is to find means of access for 'non-art historians' and 'to articulate these needs *before* any cataloguing or indexing effort is undertaken.'

Besides the Bodleian Scheme for extracting information from more
59

literary materials, the Scottish National Portrait Gallery has set up a Social History Index to cover as many as possible of the items on the pictures in its possession. Set up in 1974 by Dr Rosalind Marshall, the Index makes it possible, through a manual system, to trace details of clothing, domestic interiors and other items on the Gallery's pictures, including many photographs of originals that are elsewhere.(6)

None of the major picture libraries appear to be organised in such a way that indices of this sort could be extracted, even in principle. Because of their size and in some cases also their history, they are arranged according to general subject categories, with details residing in the heads of individuals and normally developed according to what has been termed 'demand classification'.(7) The privately owned collections are not normally open to outsiders to peruse, but are generally of easy access to those who work on them. The large general collections are all arranged by subjects, making no attempt to distinguish between photographs, lithographs, and even pages torn from magazines.

The BBC Hulton Picture Library is divided into Portraits, Topographical, Historical and Modern. The latter two sections are subdivided into a series of three-letter subheadings like EDU for Education, with other subdivisions below that. The collection has some cross-references, though there is little on the detail of the pictures.(8) The Mansell Collection is arranged according to a similar scheme with subheadings such as HOM for Home Life subdivided with a detail which varies as a function of use and quantity. WAR can be searched entirely by dates, but this does not apply in other sub-sections. Separate card indexes are kept for Cats, Ambassadors and other such topics that are commonly sought. The Mary Evans Picture Library relies on a somewhat shorter series of general headings such as Events, Daily life, Sport and Entertainment, and on rather more subdivisions within them. Some of the cross-referring is done by simply putting another copy of pictures elsewhere.

It is rare for picture libraries to be as general as these. There is much to be learnt from smaller specialist institutions. A good example is the Imperial War Museum which has over six million photographs from the first and second world wars, as well as many other pictures of various kinds.(9) Much of the visual material is already arranged as a record before even arriving at the Museum, so can easily be fitted in by campaign and battlefront, and by variations in form of military technology. There are a few subject headings also like Agriculture, Housing and Women's Work. The films, including propoganda material and unedited footage, are described in some detail in a computer based technical control system called APPARAT (Archival Preservation Programme and Retrieval by Automatic Techniques) aimed as much to aid preservation as to record content. The 9000 paintings and 50,000 posters in the

Museum are largely arranged by artist, and in some cases by country. This makes their organisation of limited interest for the present discussion.

Some general schemes

One of the few specialist institutions which aims to arrange its material according to a comprehensive subject is the Prints and Drawings Department of the Victoria and Albert Museum. This has a special index, which was constructed by Elizabeth Glass, a former Senior Research Assistant in the Department, based on the experience of the range of subject enquiries made, and aims to provide 'a scaffolding of themes and motifs under which the subject matter of a particular item is to be entered'.(10) Each picture is given a number followed by five or six subject categories. Some are quite general, such as Trades and Occupations and Ecclesiastical Architecture. Behind these are individual types within each group. Thus 'Religion and Ritual: Non-conformist Sects' are further subdivided by the names of individual groups. The entire second volume of the published index is devoted to cross-references from the various titles used. Another way into the material is by means of a topographical card index. This is certainly a most comprehensive method of granting access to pictures, and is capable of infinite refinement. The arguments against it are that it is cumbersome, involves much clerical effort, and does not necessarily apply to more specialised collections in particular fields.

Something similar to the effort at comprehensive divisions can be seen in a number of schemes that have been developed to organise collections of picture postcards beyond more obvious categories based on chronology, topography and so forth. In the 1920s and 30s a number of proposed listings were produced, some based on such abstract headings as Humour and Political, and others concentrating on items shown such as Maps, Flags, Suburban Views and Pageants.(11) Some more recent systems have used more general abstract categories like Reality, Imagination and Eroticism. It is perhaps because of the failure to refine such methods of organising the unpretentious images usually found on postcards that few serious studies of the meaning of this popular art have got beyond George Orwell's classic study of 1942. Orwell indicates, though admittedly on a narrow range of subject matter, the 'ideological meaning' of picture postcards in the enforcement of 'a fairly strict moral code', and shows how they reflect the development of private attitudes and political opinions.(12)

Since the time of Orwell's essay, the growing market in postcard collection and exchange has meant that though listings have grown more complex, they concentrate in particular on the commercial value of items, and arrangement by well-known artists and publishers.(13)

It is perhaps not surprising that few of the many books produced since Orwell's day have been able to tell us much about the meaning of the images they often profusely illustrate.

Other efforts to provide more specialised subject headings have not proved more successful. The well-kept photographs of one private business are nevertheless kept under categories either very general or very particular to the business itself.(14) On the other hand, the largest catalogue of British photograph collections suffers from too many separate categories, insufficiently defined. It nevertheless remains an essential starting point in any effort to find pictures, even when it needs to be supplemented by other more general guides.(15)

The methods of the future

In order to help researchers find pictures, it would be necessary to aim at the comprehensiveness of the Glass Index, but with added flexibility and the ability to be brought up to date. It is essential to go beyond compiling lists in order to provide useful modes of entry. It is clear that librarians and archivists are generally becoming aware of this, as one clear-minded account sets out very well.(16) 'While most people regard photographs as valuable purely in terms of providing illustrations to go with the text, it is becoming more and more apparent that these photographs should be considered as something more. It is possible to think of old (and indeed not so old) photographs in the same way as manuscript documents. Much as a great deal of information can be gleaned from manuscripts by reading between the lines, we can find much more in photographs than the photographer originally intended to capture. Since many aspects of life not normally considered as subjects for the photographer have been captured, as it were, by accident, the collections must be useful to many researchers in a variety of subject areas. The problem is, of course, to find ways in which all this information can be made available to scholars.' The writer of this article argues that although it is possible to have general descriptions, both on the level of collections and of individual pictures, there are various means of going beyond this. He goes on to propose a comparison between the Dewey numerical classification scheme applied to pictures, and an alphabetical index based on the one used for the BBC News. He mentions the possibility of computerised retrieval systems, though not the way they make it possible to get out of the limitations imposed by standardised systems of classification.

There are however, distinct signs of a new approach in this field which opens new possibilities in the organisation of pictures, and in granting access to them. The Information Retrieval Group of the Museums Association (IRGMA) emerged as an independently functioning

62

body in 1974. Since then it has carried through a great deal of theoretical and practical activity in documenting the contents of museums in Britain, and developed the Museum Documentation Unit housed at Duxford in Cambridgeshire.(17)

The GOS computer package now being used by the MDA includes much visual and other material and emphasises retrieval through generated indexes. It uses a series of standard cards which convey a wide range of information either from key words or brief summaries. Already a version of this system has been taken up by the Gas Industry in its Panel for the History of the Industry Location System (PHILIS).

The great advantage of working in this way in the organisation of information on pictures over for example the Dutch DIALS system or the Elizabeth Glass Index, is that it allows categories to develop with need and use. The main disadvantages of the MDA system are the expense of the computer used and the amount of clerical labour still involved in filling in cards and processing the data in other ways. However, technological changes on the frontiers of computer development might make it possible to process the information more easily and more cheaply, perhaps by voice reproduction or visual scanning of acquisition lists.

There is much to be learnt about the organisation of images from work that has been done in museums and art galleries throughout the world. Besides the comprehensive Dutch system that has been mentioned, the Canadian public archives have for some years operated a system which allows the retrieval of a wide range of individual items either manually or by computer. The 'Bodleian project' on manuscripts and early books clearly has much to tell about cataloguing images. The general result of discussion and experience in the field, both in France and at the MDA, shows that it is perfectly possible to utilise ordinary language in ways in which abstract ideas and general information can be retrieved from pictures.(18) The way in which such work can be developed is shown by the Joint Working Party of the Library Association, the Museums Association and the Society of Archivists which is already considering ways of making compatible the IRGMA based computer systems and the PROSPEC system which has been tried in some county archives.(19)

Nor will the use of computers necessarily provide a panacea for all the problems of recording and retrieving words and images. They may be too expensive, or too complicated. But their procedures can serve to concentrate minds on standardised means of solving problems. Any central record could operate on many levels and be as wide or deep as resources will allow. It could go from the best of all possible worlds, where every detail on every picture could be retrieved, down to general descriptions and categories. These are clearly the lines along which any further progress will be made.

NOTES TO CHAPTER SIX

1 Yeats, W B 'The circus animals' desertion' (1939) in *Collected Poems* 1950, p392.

2 Panofsky, E *Meaning in the visual arts* Penguin edition, 1970 p51.

3 Van de Wall, H *Decimal index of the art of the Low Countries* 1968, Fogg Art Museum *Photographic and slide classification for western art* Cambridge, Massachusetts, 1973 contains some subject headings, but they are very general.

4 Roberts, Helene E 'The image library', *ARLIS Journal* III 4 Winter 1978, 26, 31.

5 Ohlgren, T H 'The Bodleian Project: computer cataloguing and indexing medieval illuminated manuscripts and early printed books' in *First international conference on automatic processings of art history data and documents* I Pisa, 1978. The proceedings of this conference provide a virtual treasure trove on all the questions to be considered here, and is hereafter referred to as *APDD*.

6 Marshall, Rosalind K 'Sources for Scottish local history 3. The Scottish National Portrait Gallery' in *Local history* 11, 7, 1975 and 'The SNPG indexing system' in *Costume* (forthcoming).

7 Evans, H *The art of picture research* Newton Abbot, 1979, 77.

8 See Gibbs-Smith, C H 'The Hulton picture post library' *Journal of documentation* VI 1950 and Moss, Daphnie *Pictures: the Radio Times Hulton picture library*, Aslib: Audio Visual Workshop May 7th-8th, 1970, 1971. This institution now prefers to be known as the BBC Hulton Picture Library.

9 The general organisation and main categories are set out in an article by Jane Carmichael called 'The Imperial War Museum, London' in *Der Archivar* November 1978. A briefer summary is in the *Imperial War Museum Handbook* 1976. See also Smither, R 'Using APPARAT: cataloguing film and sound recordings at the Imperial War Museum'. *Aslib proceedings* 31(4) April 1979.

10 Glass, Elizabeth *A subject index of the visual arts* HMSO, 1969, Volume 1 iii.

11 Scott, W J *All about postcards* Leeds, 1903, 93 gives perhaps the earliest efforts and more comprehensive ones are to be found in Renieu, L *La Carte Postale illustrée, considerée au point de vue des arts Graphiques et des sujets representes* Brussels, 1924; Cole, G W *Postcards. The world in miniature. A plan for their systematic arrangement. With an index* Pasadena, California, 1935.

12 Kyron, A *L'age d'or de la carte postale* Paris, 1966; Orwell, G 'The art of Donald McGill' in *Collected essays, journalism and letters* II Penguin edition, 1970, 183-95.

13 See for example, Smith, J H D *IPM catalogue of printed postcards*

1976 (and other editions) and Hewlett, H R *Picton's priced catalogue of British pictorial postcards* 4th edition 1977.

14 Wilson, R 'The storage of photographic records' *Business archives* 40, June 1974; Godfrey, H 'The archives of J Sainsbury Limited' *Ibid*, 44, November 1978, 24.

15 Wall, J R *Directory of British photographic collections* 1977; Evans, H and M *The picture researchers handbook* 1979 edition.

16 Brunt, Rodney M 'On the development of an analytical indexing system for photographic collections', *Irish archives bulletin* 5, 1975, 25.

17 The Unit has published a great deal about its activities in *MDA news, MDA information* and elsewhere. From the point of view of the problems discussed here, the most important sources are Roberts, D A *The IRGMA retrieval system (Part 1)* January 1976; Porter, M F, Light, R B and Roberts, D A *A unified approach to the computerisation of museum catalogues* BL R&D Report 5338 HC, December 1976; Light, R 'Today's technology recording the past' *Computing Europe* 3 November 1977, 25; Porter, M F and Roberts, D A 'The work of the Museum Documentation Association with fine art and photographic data recording' *APDD I* (see n5); MDA *Pictorial representation card instructions* June 1979; Roberts, D A and Light, R B 'Museum documentation' *Journal of documentation* March 1980.

18 Delisle, G 'La recherche par l'image' *APDD I*; n5 above; Preand, M and Rio, M 'Images sans historie. Methode de description des images et classement informatique' *APDD II 245.*

19 See the Joint Working Party's Statement of Policy Relating to Archives of 1978.

CHAPTER SEVEN

NON-BOOK MATERIALS IN HOUSING

The White Rabbit put on his spectacles. 'Where shall I begin, please Your Majesty?' he asked.
'Begin at the beginning,' the King said, very gravely, 'and go on till you come to the end: then stop.'

Lewis Carrol
Alice in Wonderland Chapter 12

In order to consider non-book printed materials of a completely different sort, it was thought necessary to look at what is available for the study of a 'modern social problem'. The 'problem' chosen was housing both because of the complex network of institutions that produce, consume and retain information in this field, and because it is not adequately covered in any of the central sources. For purposes of this survey an arbitrary line was drawn to exclude technological and other aspects of the subject. However, in following the advice of Alice's King of Hearts, and setting out from the beginning the sources of information in the field, a number of important points became clear. Firstly, the 'ephemera' category broke down almost immediately when materials from single sheets of paper to substantial 'near print' pamphlets and computer tapes were considered. In looking at the collections themselves it proved even more absurd to look at the books, pamphlets, leaflets and reports they contained, and to pick out those which could merely be defined by their form.

The second point that stood out was that the arrangement of the materials in the sorts of collections being considered here, was usually quite different from the 'historical' and 'pictorial' parts of the survey, where the sources listed could largely be said to be set out in 'dead' or, at least, 'formed' collections. This time the materials that had to be considered were of a kind that appears and disappears every day. They were found to be arranged in ways that might alter drastically at any time or simply disappear into waste paper baskets or shredding machines.

66

In the end it was necessary to go beyond the category of 'collections', well beyond the printed word and into information gathering which included oral contacts and the concerns of individual advice and social work. Not only did it become artificial to think in terms of printed paper, but it was also necessary to approach individuals and 'contacts' in order to complete each part of the information network.

The third point that became clear was that, once these problems had been resolved, it was not difficult even for a novice in the field to carry out the King's advice to the White Rabbit and to 'go on till you come to the end: then stop'. It proved quite possible to move into a 'network' of organisations and contacts, to be passed from one to another without any great effort on one's own part, and after three or four months to get to a point where the people and institutions then approached could only advise turning back to those who had already been seen, listed and described. Furthermore, it can be shown that it was possible to move through the particular set of networks in this study, and to gather more knowledge about the information sources within it than are available to any individual at a particular point. By the nature of things, every single individual and organisation in so vast a field could not be listed, but it can be claimed that the list which is set out in Appendix Seven makes it possible to enter into the major networks. The paragraphs that follow describe how this was done. These are supplemented by Appendix Seven, which sets out the main sources, and the following chapter discusses some of the general issues that arise in making a central record of material of this sort.

National organisations

To begin at the beginning in the field of housing is to go to the largest producer and organiser of information, which is the Department of the Environment. The Department's library produces a series of bibliographical publications jointly with the Department of Transport.(1) The Library contains the largest extant collection of structure plans and other planning and housing materials nearly all in 'near print' form and published in limited editions by all local authorities. It naturally collects all of the official publications of the Environment Department itself, going beyond HMSO publications, press releases and so forth, but not necessarily including everything that comes out from all the far flung activities of every part of the Department. The *Annual list of publications* sets out details not only of HMSO and general Departmental publications and circulars, but also Acts, statutory instruments, and the material being produced by associated research establishments and similar bodies, down to isolated reports and articles. The *Library bulletin* produced every month contains abstracts of periodical articles, and the library catalogue, which has been printed for the period 1943-77 is also a major source of information. The various bibliographical and other guides produced by the library are largely summaries of these other publications.

It would be possible to mention numerous other national bodies, linked directly or indirectly to the machinery of government, but it does not seem likely that they could be said to include anything of significance that cannot be found in the Library of the Department itself. The Building Research Establishment, for example, covers construction research, dealing with housing and housing installations. Its publications are all summarised in those of the DoE Library and more is to be found from its annual *Information directory*.(2) The Housing Corporation was set up in 1964 to promote cost rent and copartnership housing, particularly by encouraging and supervising housing associations. Although its own information resources are not extensive, the corporation publishes a great deal of general relevance to the field. Some examples are given in Appendix Seven, entry 3.

A number of organisations independent of government exist whose purpose it is to provide information about housing and allied subjects. Probably the most well known of these is the Housing Centre Trust. This is an independent body founded in 1934, funded by affiliates that include public authorities and aiming 'to provide a link between individuals and organisations and to encourage the free interchange of ideas on all aspects of housing'. To this end, it brings out various publications, runs a library, organises seminars and visits and generally provides a centre for information distribution in the field. It is perhaps worth mentioning that although its library and publications are entirely 'books' by most of the conventional definitions, the Secretary is well able to provide access to many forms of less conventional 'periodical publications' and ephemera of a more obvious kind.(3) A large amount of recent report literature and similar material was to be found in the same building at the Centre for Environmental Studies, but this is now wound up as part of government cuts of so-called 'quangos'. The Institute of Housing, although it does not itself contain a great deal of information, organises research and study within the field.

Research bodies
Information and research in this subject is also carried out by a number of bodies within universities. Two of the most important of these are in Birmingham and Bristol, and information about them is found in Appendix Seven entries 7 and 8. These entries are not intended to be complete accounts of the institutions in the field, but representative samples of what exist; providing a means of entry to this particular part of the network. A general service of such information is provided by Capital Planning Information Limited to subscribers, and details

are given in Appendix Seven, entry 9. Other specialist bodies deal with information provision in particular parts of the housing field. One of these is the Housing Information Service which produced *Housing abstracts* covering the voluntary housing association sector. Another part of the field is covered by the Self-Help Housing Resource Library which at the time of this research in November 1979 was located in the Polytechnic of North London and contained a great deal of valuable information not covered elsewhere. Financed until April 1979 by the Gulbenkin Foundation, it is now facing some uncertainty about its future, of a sort discussed more fully in the next chapter.

Local authorities
General information about housing is also available from the local authorities responsible for its administration. Conspicuous in this respect is the Intelligence Department of the Greater London Council, which performs functions well beyond even the vast scope of housing in the metropolis. The Department produces a bewilderingly wide range of research aids, current awareness reports and summaries of books, pamphlets and much else besides. The Research Library also includes a file of internally generated GLC material, a slide library and an on-line retrieval system known as ACOMPLIS (A Computerised London Information Service) which covers the London boroughs as well as the GLC. It also has a computer terminal that allows it to subscribe to a number of commercially available bibliographical data bases. Two other interesting features are efforts to incorporate student dissertations into the information base, and the relative lack of interest in anything more than three or four years old. Though relations were not always entirely amicable in the past, a steady flow of 'used' material now goes to the quite separate archival services of the Council. Outside official sources there is no systematic acquisition policy by the library, nor could there be with the lack of any centralised record of the multifarious publications of university departments, pressure groups and a wide range of other bodies.

It is not surprising that very few other local authorities have anything like the same range of materials and publications. Thus for example in Birmingham the Housing Department does some abstracting for its own internal purposes, but relies on such sources as *Urban abstracts*, working closely with the Public Library system. There is similar cooperation in the London Borough of Camden, which also has a Housing Information Officer who has attempted to improve the work of the Council.(4) The Local Government Information Project at Sheffield's School of Librarianship has discovered a limited use of such facilities in at least one housing department.(5) Efforts to pool information resources amongst local authorities on a regional basis have

69

apparently had more fruitful results in the North West of England. A more permanent, and clearly very effective means of such work has been the Planning Exchange in Glasgow, originally initiated in 1972 by the Centre for Environmental Studies. This collects and provides information in housing and related fields not only to local authorities but also to official bodies, pressure groups and others. It now describes itself as 'an independent body funded mainly by local authorities and central government in Scotland, as an information centre for new developments in environmental and social planning and a central service point for local authorities and related agencies'. It 'does not take sides on issues but tries to act as an honest broker between different interests and backgrounds'. It issues an *Information bulletin* and various other publications, runs courses and in various ways pools information in the field. It remains the only permanent institution of its kind in the British Isles.(6) Local authorities have themselves taken recently to publishing information on their policies including housing. Both Lambeth and Islington in London for example, produce tabloid bulletins called *News* informing tenants of their rights and of the policies of the respective councils. A wide variety of similar tabloid-style publications are produced by various departments of the Strathclyde Regional authority.

Local government documentation and publication presents its own particular set of problems which have been considered in recent works paralleled to this by Mr Don Kennington and Capital Planning Information, and by Mr Barry Nuttall of Leeds Polytechnic.(7) It is to be hoped that steps in the direction of a more standardised and centralised system of access to publications from this source will be the result.

Housing Aid Centres, of which around two-thirds are in what may be termed the local authority sector, also have their own network of information and contacts.(8) The Association of Housing Aid in Birmingham, which brings together not the formal bodies themselves, but those who work in them and support their aims, publishes bulletins and regular material about their work.(9) A publication called *HAC abstracts* is produced by the London Borough of Camden Housing Aid Centre, and is of general relevance to those working in this sector. Examples of aid centre publications of more local relevance are *Tall stories* published by the Deptford Housing Aid Centre and *HARU news* published by the Housing Advice Resource Unit in the London borough of Southwark.

Specialist institutions
It would also be possible to set out details of information in many other of the far flung sectors of this vast field. For example, attention could be drawn to the publications of the building societies, the statistical

and other information in the Building Society's Association *BSA bulletin* and the briefer more popular and well-known *Housing trends* published by the Nationwide Building Society and backed by a specialised library. The Bristol and West Building Society produces a more general *Housing outlook*, an occasional magazine. In another part of the market there is the Society of Cooperative Dwellings which produces *Scoop*, a regular monthly newsletter. The voluntary sector also has its own network of information resources and contacts. There is a National Federation of Housing Associations that keeps up with news in the field. Individual associations may well be the best information gatherers and providers, to judge from the Family Housing Association which employs a full time librarian and information officer. This is said to be the only one with such facilities, in London at least.

Pressure groups
In going beyond this to the well-known national pressure groups in the field of housing deprivation, one is struck by the contrasts in information organisation and provision. At Shelter—the National Campaign for the Homeless—the amount of information held on paper is quite large including numbers of pamphlets and press cuttings, some from an agency. Bibliographies are produced for specific internal purposes and the photograph library is used for publicity. Nevertheless it is clear that Shelter is more concerned with public relations and with press coverage for its campaigns than with the provision of detailed information. Thus a good deal of the material on which its publications and activities are based come from the Westminster Reference Library and the London School of Economics. SHAC, the London Housing Aid Centre, which is often confused with Shelter, performs a different set of functions. It is not directly a campaigning body, but is mainly involved in taking up individual cases. Unlike Shelter it is largely dependent on public funds. It has less in the way of information resources than Shelter, but they are rather more carefully organised. Details of this are given in Appendix Seven. A third major national pressure group is CHAR, the Campaign for Single Homeless People, set up in 1973. CHAR mainly acts as a pressure group, but also passes people on to agencies offering accommodation and takes a specific responsibility for publishing research and information in its particular field. It has a good collection of pamphlets, newspaper cuttings and other relevant materials. Similar general functions are performed by CHAS, the Catholic Housing Aid Society, which organises local aid centres and publications on a more comprehensive basis than its name might imply.

Local and community information provision
One other important source for the provision of housing information
lies through the library and information facilities of local authorities.
A few years ago there would have been little to say about services
provided by this means. Activities in the field have however expanded
greatly in recent years under the influence of a new generation of
young librarians, eager to provide information to their communities
instead of just collecting books. This development and how it has
worked out in different cases has been the subject of a recent research
project undertaken at Leeds Polytechnic.(10) Another study is the
Community Information Project financed by the BL R&D Department
and based at the Library Association, which has considered further
developments of the subject, and produced two most useful publications.(11)

With so much research in a large and complex field already under
way it is difficult here to do more than present examples of the sorts of
efforts made to collect local housing information. In 'person based'
rather than book or 'document based' services, quite different sets of
criteria apply. In all cases ephemeral literature, leaflets, pamphlets and
periodicals relevant to housing and kept for distribution rather than
collection are used in association with individual advice and contacts.
Amongst examples of this form of activity is the Longsight 'Community
Information Library', which is part of what appears to be the only
building of any modernity or elegance amongst the more familiar
manifestations of urban decay close to the centre of Manchester. From
here a well organised system of dispensing information operates in
collaboration with the local Citizens Advice Bureau, the Law Centre
and 'community' organisations. Readers looking for more conventional
research facilities are sent to the Central Library two miles up the road.
Current information, mostly in the form of ephemeral publications,
is easily available and there is a lively young staff whose work is com-
mended by local councillors who themselves use the facilities. The
ephemeral material, of which there is a great deal (though little which
could truly be described as local), is only there to be used during the
period when it is current, after which it is thrown away. Similar
material is arranged in packs for general distribution throughout the
libraries in Peterborough, while in Cheshire 'information centres'
using and distributing this material operate quite separately from the
library system. Very little of the material used in these activities
appears in the *British national bibliography*, and none at all in *The
bookseller*. A large proportion of it, for housing at least, is of course
produced by bodies which have already been mentioned in this survey.
(12)

Many of the problems of developing these services derive from the
72

need to get over previously existing institutional dividing lines. There seems to be general agreement now amongst those in the public library service of the need for some at least of their profession to provide 'person based' services and not to spend too long worrying about the 'often unfruitful debate on the extent to which libraries give advice in answering enquiries'.(13) Problems however remain at the cross roads between governmental and semi-governmental agencies, and this can be seen by considering the information providing aspects of the work of Citizens Advice Bureaux. The National Federation of CAB provides a comprehensive series of packs, which are files of material, about half written specially to explain aspects of the work of local bureaux. The rest of the material consists of various leaflets and pamphlets, mostly official, considered to be adequate for what they cover. The packs are frequently brought up to date. Though they increasingly go to the public libraries they are not normally on public display there, since they are intended to be mediated through expert advisers who know how to follow up references and to contact further sources. Those at the National Federation responsible for producing and distributing this information are unhappy with the possibility that it might be inexpertly used.(14) Another network of organisations that straddle somewhat uneasily the dividing line of official and unofficial are the housing aid centres. Some of these began as arms of local government; others are under the auspices of Shelter, or CHAS, or else are independent voluntary organisations. They help people find places to live. Their need for centralised information is desperate. Efforts to take steps in this direction have not proved very effective, in London at least, though a National Association has been set up and a Directory issued.(15)

Alternative information networks
The biggest difficulty for information provision in this sector lies in the responsibility and paying for information needs which may come into conflict with established authorities. This problem is described more fully in the next chapter, but for the moment it is possible to notice the proliferation over the past few years of a series of institutions that do not feel themselves subject to any such restraints. The development of local information and resource centres for tenants, women, trade unionists and others has been part of the expansion of 'community politics' of many kinds. These are often in association with public or semi-public bodies like neighbourhood and housing advice centres, consumer advice centres and law centres, or on the other hand with organisations of tenants, squatters, shop stewards, women, racial minorities and others. A common pattern in the development of local resource and information centres has been their establishment, either from public funds to fulfill vague aims of social amelioration often

with support from the Manpower Services Commission, or a private charity like the Rowentree or Gulbenkian foundations. They have then taken on a life of their own, with public authorities cutting off funding and charitable institutions not prepared to provide finance beyond the 'pilot' stage. They have often then continued to exist on a shoestring provided by the local pressure groups and their less wealthy bodies for whom they provide a useful service. The twelve community development projects set up in 1968 to take up the questions of inner city decay became troublesome offspring of the public authorities who created them, undertaking increasingly 'anti-establishment' activities and publications. All funding was withdrawn from them in 1978 and they were said to have been actively obstructed by the Home Office during 1979.(16)

These problems have resulted in the dissemination of non-official materials which have been tackled by a number of agencies, mostly semi-commercial, that have grown up in recent years. Material on housing produced by voluntary organisations, pressure groups and local bodies are sent out by the Publications Distribution Cooperative based in London, and Scottish and Northern Books in Hebden Bridge. Though this includes some of what might be called 'near print', and some from institutions which may only produce one or two publications during their entire lives, on the whole it comes in conventional book and periodical format. Nevertheless, virtually nothing of what the PDC deals with gets into *The bookseller*, so an alternative *Radical bookseller* has been appearing, somewhat irregularly, since the end of 1979. PDC material mostly goes out, in the first place at least, through the well-known network of 'alternative' bookshops such as 'Grass Roots' in Manchester and the 'Corner Bookshop' in Leeds. Associated with this is 'Campaign Books' in central London, which goes to some lengths to stock materials from pressure groups of all kinds and as well as selling it, attempts to distribute it through libraries.(17)

Beyond the network of distribution and sales, it is possible to say something of the wide and varied forms of local information provision, much of it of very recent growth. Some aspects of the development of information provision within the public library sector have already been mentioned, and some examples of the pattern of development and funding have been mentioned. Numerous other variants could be set out, giving means of entry into networks of many kinds. Thus the more 'established' voluntary sector has for some time been concerned with the deficiencies in local information provision.(18) Between 1975 and 1977 a number of resource centres were set up to aid the work of such voluntary organisations, partly though not entirely for the purpose of more efficient information provision. A study has recently been published covering a number of these.(19) This covers

74

the Britich Council Community Work Resource Unit, the Govan Area Resource Centre, the London Voluntary Service Council Community Work Service, the Manchester Area Resource Centre, the South Wales Anti-Poverty Action Centre, and the Tyne and Wear Resource Centre. It would not be difficult to present a long list of such institutions with origins and activities as varied. They normally regarded themselves as part of 'alternative' information networks, opposed to the established authorities, including public libraries, and see themselves as more flexible and responsive to the needs of local communities. The holdings of a number of these bodies in the housing field were found to be quite extensive. The Coventry Workshop, which began in 1975 and is perhaps the most well established, has one of the most extensive stocks of local information in the field of housing. It works with the Coventry Resource and Information Centre (CRIS) whose printed holdings are less extensive, but is more concerned with general political campaigning and taking up individual cases. The Tyne and Wear Resources Centre since beginning in March 1979 has collected general material in the field and issues a number of large scale publications.(20) The Trade Union and Community Resource and Information Centre was set up in Leeds in May 1978 with a staff that included a trained librarian. Like the Tyne and Wear body, it has cooperated with local trades councils in the distribution of material on local housing conditions and has also brought out a useful publication on local structure plans, as well as a local bibliography on health and safety which could no doubt be emulated in a number of other fields.(21) Although the problem of future funding exists for all these bodies, many will no doubt continue through a combination of individual enthusiasm, some support from charitable foundations and income from affiliations.

Efforts to develop information networks have taken many forms. Local trade union organisations have in some cases been part of efforts which developed out of the Community Development Projects and Workshop bodies to which reference has been made. However, on the whole such bodies have been slow to develop information facilities, despite the beginnings of discussions on the matter, and the setting up during 1979 of a Trade Union Information Group.(22) There is more promise perhaps in general 'anti-establishment' agencies allying themselves to community groups, women's groups, trade unions and others.(23) It may be possible to develop also the model provided by general local information networks, or to provide information through the more 'established' voluntary network.(24) No doubt it will eventually be possible to make use of the imaginative techniques developed largely for commercial concerns in the well-known scheme in the London Borough of Lambeth.(25)

To have arrived at this point might seem to have taken the effort to

75

list 'collections of ephemera' a long way from its starting point in the John Johnson Collection and in the world of libraries, archives and museums in which it began. For reasons which it is hoped have become clear, the list of 'collections' given at the end of the chapter cannot claim to be complete. Nor can it claim to encompass 'ephemera collections' in any purist sense. It can claim, however, to include a wide range of examples that are both important and typical. Above all, it can be shown that it has been possible to enter all the important networks in such a way that a serious researcher could be launched into a position of pursuing all the major categories of information that exist. Some of the remaining problems that have been referred to are discussed in the following chapter.

NOTES TO CHAPTER SEVEN

1 The most important of these publications for purposes of the present study is Connolly, Kathleen *Sources of information in housing* 1st ed 1975, 2nd ed February 1979. Though it has not been possible to compile as comprehensive a list in this Report, it has not been difficult to cover some of the most important examples more comprehensively, and to deal more fully with the 'anti-establishment' sector. Also very comprehensive in Ellender, Pat *Housing in Britain. A select list relating to housing* July 1979 including summaries of many periodical articles. Kidd, Susan *New towns in Britain* September 1977 and Pugh, Hilary *Housing co-operatives and co-partnership schemes* August 1976 also give long lists of books and articles. The first of these is from an *Information series* issued by the DoE Library, and the others are from a *Bibliography series*. There is also an *Occasional papers series*. Separate lists are available of currently available examples in these lists, though some are rather dated and many do not relate to housing.

2 This gives summaries of literature, sources of publications and details of other organisations, including for example the Building Centres, of which a large source is the one at 26 Store Street, London WC1. There are others in most main towns.

3 Housing Centre Bookshop *Catalogue of British housing books in print* 1978. The Trust has also published Smith, Mary E H *A guide to housing* 2nd ed 1977 and brings out a bi-monthly *Housing review*.

4 For details see Orna, M 'Blueprint for an information service' in *Housing* November 1979.

5 'GMF' *Use of the Bweltin Leywodraeth Leol in the County of Gwynedd* Project Logi Research Note 23, October 1979.

6 Preson, T 'GREMLIN: a co-operative local government information service' *Aslib proceedings* May 31, 1979; *The planning Exchange Scotland. A guide to its organisation and services* Glasgow, 1980.

7 Nuttall, B S *Organisation and control of local government documentation* BL R&D Report February 1980.

8 Mylan, D *Housing aid and advice centres* Association of Housing Aid, Birmingham 1979 gives details of the working of these centres and of publications about them.

9 Among interesting material available from the centre is Birmingham Housing Aid Service *Report on the service's work 1977 and 1978.*

10 Watson, Joyce, Bowen, Judith and Walley, E D *The management of community information services in the public library* Leeds Polytechnic, March 1979. This includes a full bibliography. See also Bowen, Judith *The design implementation of a community information service in the library* Leeds Polytechnic, September 1978 which describes the establishment of a service at Bretton, near Peterborough. The development of new attitudes within the library profession can be traced for example in Hackman, P 'Public librarians, information and the community' in *Assistant librarian* February 1973 and Jordan, P 'Librarians and social commitment' *Ibid* April 1975. See also Bunch, A *More than just books: a short guide to community information in libraries* Library Association, 1979, and Darcy, B and Ohri, A *Libraries are ours. The public library as a source of information for community groups* Community Projects Foundation, 1979.

11 They are *Knowhow. A guide to information, training and campaigning materials for information and advice workers* 1979 compiled by Grainne Morby and edited by Elaine Kempson, and *Community information. What libraries can do* Library Association, 1980, which can be used to expand the information contained in succeeding paragraphs.

12 There is an unpublished paper on these questions by Allen Bunch entitled *Bibliographical control and acquisition of community information source material.*

13 Watson, J et al *op cit*, 111, 115.

14 Forrest, R 'Help me if you can . . . the role of the Citizens' Advice Bureaux in the information network' *Assistant librarian* October 1975, advocates closer cooperation, and an interesting letter in *Ibid* January 1976, 14 suggests that the lack of such cooperation in the past has not always been the fault of librarians.

15 Mylan, Dave *Directory of housing aid and advice centres* Association of Housing Aid, Birmingham March 1979.

16 For details see *The radical bookseller* 2 November 1979.

17 For more details see Kearns, C 'Out of the mainstream' in *Assistant librarian* February 1980. Kearns rightly mentions *News from Neasden* which appears somewhat irregularly, mostly with lists of radical books.

18 Community Work Group *Current issues in community work* 1973, 134.

19 Lees, Ray and Bailey, Nick *Interim report on six resource centres October 1979. Origins; objectives; organisation* Polytechnic of Central London, 1979.

20 See for example, Tyne and Wear Resource Centre *Demolishing the myths, housing and jobs in South Tyneside* 1979.

21 Leeds Trades Council *Which way home? A report on housing in Leeds* November 1978; TUCRIC *A critical guide to reading the West Yorkshire structure plan* Autumn 1978; Oxley, M *Health and safety. Information sources in Leeds* TUCRIC, June 1979.

22 Backhouse, Roger 'Library services to trade unions ignored or forgotten?' *Assistant librarian* December 1977. Mr Backhouse of the Bow Library, London E3 is the moving spirit of the TUIG. For a more detailed account of what currently exists see Foster, J and Hodgson, K 'New directions: the need for local research resources in the Labour Movement' in *The state and the local economy*, published by the Community Development Project Economy Collective in 1979.

23 See for example London Labour Library *Public information. A directory of information sources for trade unionists and campaign groups* October 1979.

24 Asser, M 'Information and advisory services: the Leicestershire experiences' *New library world* June 1974.

25 LINK *Directory of members* 1972; O'Rourke, E 'LINK: the Lambeth information network' *Assistant librarian* July 1974; London Voluntary Service Council *Monitoring the cuts: who is doing what?* February 1980.

CHAPTER EIGHT

GOVERNMENTS, LIBRARIANS AND PRESSURE GROUPS

The (National Document Library) should be responsible for compiling a national register of collections of research material in the social sciences, for publishing a newsletter and operating a referral service based on this register, and for advising the National Central Library on the most appropriate libraries to which material offered for deposit might be directed. Compilation of such a register is, indeed, a matter of urgency and should be initiated in anticipation of the recommended structure.

> John E. Pemberton
> *The national provision of printed ephemera in the Social Sciences*
> University of Warwick 1971 p47.

The solution proposed a decade ago by John Pemberton to a somewhat narrower set of problems than have been considered in this book will be discussed once again in greater detail in the concluding chapter. In the meantime it is necessary to show that the questions under consideration in the present work have led inevitably, over the years, to the same general conclusion.

The multifarious forms and locations of documentation encountered in the final part of the research set out in this book, covering the field of housing information, present more complicated problems than in the first two parts of the project, though they are not different in kind. The forms of material being currently used in the housing field are much more varied, its location less permanent, and the need for its use more immediate. Nevertheless it is possible to make similar general points about collection, organisation and location.

Many publications seen during the course of travel around the networks in the field of housing will never get into a copyright library, or a central record of any kind. People employed by large government agencies in some cases do not even seem aware of their legal obligations. In the national voluntary sector, a recent survey found that thirty-one organisations submitted material which arrived in the British National

Bibliography. Though not all of these were primarily concerned with the housing field, they included all of those listed at the end of the previous chapter. The same survey, however, named twenty national groups where titles were not included, and also gave numerous examples (including from several organisations named in the present survey) of important publications which did not appear. The survey points out that these deficiencies arise in part at least because it is very time-consuming for British Library staff to chase up material not deposited, especially from bodies which may be new or unknown, or have limited resources available to publicise their existence.(1) This is without even being able to give more than a limited consideration to local publications and information sources of the kind considered in the closing section of the previous chapter.

These problems arise directly from the burdens placed on busy people who are not given the resources to perform the tasks placed upon them. However, there are methods of looking at their problems which can be considered in order to point to ways of resolving them.

To take first the 'official' and other such publications which were considered at the beginning of the previous chapter. One result of current government economy cuts has been that a diminishing proportion of 'official' publications have been getting such forms of standard treatment as command numbers. Furthermore, numerous publications of individual departments of state, not to mention documents that for some purposes can be regarded as 'internal' are difficult to find and retain. The ominous shadow of official secrecy casts its gloom over much serious consideration of this topic.(2) Even where this problem does not arise, rivalries between different sections of any bureaucratic apparatus can prevent material from seeing the light of day when there is no other special reason why it should not. There are those in the British Library and elsewhere who attempt to penetrate these problems. It should be pointed out however that from those trying to deal with such documentation within the departments of state themselves, there comes the proposal that all government-produced material which can in any way be regarded as published should be made copyright and dealt with through the machinery of the British Library. This would serve to provide at least part of the material for the 'National Documents Library' envisaged in Pemberton's report, though it must be said that it is regarded with less than enthusiasm by those with current responsibilities in the field.

The area of local government documentation presents even greater difficulties along the same lines, particularly since there is no agreed standard form of arrangement. It is to be hoped that the researches of Barry Nuttall and Don Kennington mentioned elsewhere will cast some light on how to produce standard lists of publishers, and agreed repertories for current information. Mr Nuttall's notion of a centralized agency would seem to be the only practical alternative, and the functions he envisages for such an agency could be carried out by a 'National Register of Collections' advocated in the final chapter of this book.(3)

Problems less of secrecy than of access apply to the results of research published in numerous semi-print forms. By far the largest collection of such material is to be found in the British Library Lending Division, and systematic efforts are made to collect it. However, problems do arise from making 'report literature' into a separate category, particularly outside the field of science and technology where it has its origins. There are difficulties in gaining access by subject to this mass of material with a limited list of headings. Problems of access are always posed when material is arranged by form rather than content. That is why it would seem that details of research institutions in particular would provide a valuable supplement to lists of reports such as are produced by the Lending Division of the British Library.(4) In the field of housing there certainly has been a wide selection of such literature at the Centre for Environmental Studies which will not be so well kept in the future. The list of research institutions given in the previous chapter would also allow entry into this part of the field.

One other important source of information on modern social problems is the public library service. Some discussion about materials distributed and used here have been set out in the previous chapter. The elements of the 'throw away society' in the activities of 'community information librarians', clearly limits the scope for listing fixed collections in any central source. Nevertheless this still does not mean that there can be no central record which would make it possible to record strong and particular holdings where they are, in something like the form which has been set out in Appendix Seven. The same applies to the national voluntary organisations and pressure groups. As has been shown, their information resources can be very variable, and an overall central record would allow for a great deal more cooperation than currently obtains in other matters.

One other issue in relation to the holdings of this kind is the difficult matter of paying pipers and calling tunes. Amongst the pressure groups surveyed in Chapter Seven, Shelter takes a great deal of pride from its independence of public funds. However, this fact does not seem to have any influence on the nature of its information resources, as compared to other similar bodies with different funding. (This is not to say of course that other aspects of the work of these bodies may not be affected by the form of their funding.) The public institutions, notably the Department of the Environment Library, clearly go to some lengths to collect material that is 'anti-establishment'. However, the producers of much of this literature are often ill-disposed towards the Department

81

and do not consider the presenting of their activities and findings to its library as very high in their list of priorities. This applies in particular to the multifarious local bodies.

Nor is it possible to think in terms of the public library system being entirely comprehensive in these matters. The 'community information librarians' do clearly attempt to be as comprehensive as possible in their coverage and do try to cover the activities of the powers that be as well as their opponents. However, in at least one place that was visited during this research, local councillors had objected to the availability in a public library of published leaflets that attacked aspects of the policies of the present government likely to materially affect a large number of those using the particular library. One group of researchers have agreed that the solution to this problem is to make a careful distinction between what is 'party political' or otherwise, and excluding anybody with general political aims from using the library facilities.(5)

However, the fact that the problem cannot be solved as easily as this is clearly indicated by the development of local resource centres and similar bodies, whose evolution and some of whose problems have been described in the previous chapter. The Coventry Workshop, for example, says that it aims: 'to support workers, the unemployed, tenants and residents, and their organisations, in their efforts to gain control collectively over their lives, and to understand the forces which deny them this control.' On housing, the workshop asserts that: 'while the City Council presents a picture of Coventry as a well-designed, well-built city, thousands of tenants live in appalling housing conditions as the result of the crisis. The City Council's own policies combine with the cuts imposed by national government to aggravate the situation, restricting council house building, improvement, and repairs'.(6) This set of attitudes is so very different from other holders of information in the field that it is impossible to conceive of direct co-operation with every other institution mentioned. Listing, however, would allow means of entry into this part of the network.

A central referral agency for the side range of sources is clearly needed. Such an agency has been advocated by Pemberton and others whose views are outlined in the concluding chapter. Recent research projects have shown the usefulness of providing lists of sources, including annotated accounts of what currently exists.(7) It is possible without a great deal of trouble or expense to go beyond this, and much of the final chapter will be devoted to indicating in more detail how this can be done.

NOTES TO CHAPTER EIGHT
1 Watson, Joyce *Bibliography of ephemeral community information materials. Part 2: An assessment of British national bibliography*

coverage of housing and educational titles for January 1977 to April 1979. Leeds Polytechnic, July 1979, BL R&D Report 5535.

2 Barnes, J A *Who should know what? Social Sciences, privacy and ethics* Penguin 1979, 185; Wraith, R *Open government: the British interpretation* 1977.

3 Nuttall, B S *Organisation and control of local government documentation* BL R&D Report 5566, February 1980.

4 Basic information is in the monthly British Library Lending Division *Announcement bulletin. A guide to British reports, translations and theses.*

5 Watson, Joyce, Bowen, Judith and Walley, E D *The management of community information services in the public library* Leeds Polytechnic, March 1979, 109 f.

6 Coventry Workshop *A labour and community research and advisory centre* leaflet.

7 Watson, Joyce *Bibliography of ephemeral community information materials. Part 1: A sources guide* Leeds Polytechnic July 1979, BL R&D Report 5521 especially 10-11. See also Morby, G *Knowhow. A guide to information, training and campaigning materials for information and advice workers* Community Information Project, Library Association 1979.

CHAPTER NINE

EPHEMERA COLLECTIONS:
THE PARTICULAR AND THE GENERAL

Only the ephemeral is of lasting value.
>   Eugene Ionesco
>   Improvisation or The Shepherd's Chameleon (1956)

'Never again', cried the man, 'never again will we wake up in the morning
and ask Who am I? What is my purpose in life? Does it really, cosmically
speaking *matter* if I don't get up and go to work? For today we will
finally learn once and for all the plain and simple answer to all those
nagging little problems of Life, the Universe and Everything!'
>   Douglas Adams
>   *The hitch-hiker's guide to the galaxy*
>   1979 p133.

This final chapter, like Douglas Adams' guide, will not actually be able
to provide the answer to every question in the universe of ephemera.
It is however possible to say something generally about the character of
the collections which have been surveyed and to make some general
suggestions about an overall approach to dealing with them. It should
be explained again that it has not been found possible to survey ephemeral printed material at the point of its production. To give any serious
estimate even of the size and scope of such material currently being
produced would be far beyond the capacity of a Hercules, and it is
difficult to see any useful purpose it could in the end serve.(1) Nor is it
practical to deal with the problems at the point of distribution. It is
possible to say something more about what happens to ephemeral
printed material at the point of exchange, though difficult to propose
much that could be done under the present order of things. The most
efficacious way of finding out about the printed paper that exists is to
look at it at the places where it is being collected and used. Before
setting out some of the general conclusions about dealing with such
collections, some of the main themes which emerged from the survey
itself should be reiterated.

84

Some particular problems

The questions posed in the course of this book about printed ephemera may briefly be summarised as follows. What is it? How can it be found? How is it arranged and kept? The answers to these questions which are given are not necessarily those that were expected by the author, and it has not always proved easy to justify them to those who have their own prejudices. They need therefore to be set out in summary form as plainly as possible.

The first point, emphasised from the beginning, is that there is no agreed view of the definition of the comparatively novel term 'printed ephemera'. The differences set out in the first chapter do not simply apply to the term 'ephemera'—they could have been traced in the varying starting points applying, for example, to 'records'.(2) Nevertheless, however different the problem looks from the various starting points of the interested parties, there does exist a gap in the organisation of knowledge that needs to be considered and can to some extent be filled. This has been demonstrated by the character of the detail it has been possible to bring together in the appendices, not simply on 'general ephemera collections' but also on the various sorts of materials in three sharply contrasted subject areas. In practice it may be necessary to make ad hoc dividing lines between different types of printed material which, while perfectly sensible, cannot be said to show the way to any general approach.(3) It is also possible to make progress even when it is not possible to learn 'the plain and simple answer to all those nagging little problems', no doubt because there never will be one.

Nor do the problems of dealing with printed ephemera simply derive from differences about the meaning of words. There are some excellent historical and objective reasons for the differences in the approach of librarians, museum curators, archivists and information scientists. There are actual differences of interest between custodians, collectors and users. Government agencies, private collectors and pressure groups are by the nature of things in conflict with one another well before they enter the realm of information provision. However it is to be hoped that the points made particularly in Chapters Four, Six and Eight can serve to break down some of the mutual incomprehension. It has been possible to give examples of how some public custodians could cooperate with users to make more accessible the materials in their charge. There is certainly evidence of a growing consciousness of this need, as one recent guide for archivists clearly sets it out.(4) 'There are in fact two kinds of list available to an archivist: one based upon the structure of the archives, the other based on the needs of the user ... An archivist must provide both kinds of instrument ... In practice, most users require only subject-based finding aids.' Even if this excellent advice is not always acted upon, it does reflect what is

85

nowadays aimed at. Librarians also are clearly becoming aware of the need for a subject basis in the organisation of knowledge.(5) This will remain necessary, as has been seen in earlier chapters, however many bodies there are of the sort that specialise in Agriculture at Reading and in Shoes at Northampton.

The problem of levels of descriptions and accessibility can be resolved not only by cooperation between custodians and users, but also by an imaginative attitude on the part of the custodians.(6) Thus many of the individual items described in this book, particularly in the historical and pictorial fields could only have been found in practice in institutions which at least aim to list them in as much detail as possible. The technology of word processors and character recognition by machines is proceeding so quickly that it is to be hoped that it will soon in the future enchance the availability of the printed materials of the past. It is only to be hoped that other new technology can be applied to the problems of security which exist in certain sorts of public and private collections, as well as in the more well-known and frequently discussed spheres of arrangement and conservation. Before considering how such materials could generally become more available, something should be said on the nature and form in which they are to be found.

The collections themselves

Collections of non-book printed materials seldom or never consist simply of items that might be characterised as 'ephemera' according to the definitions variously employed by librarians, archivists, museum curators and collectors. With certain important exceptions such collections always include materials which could be consigned other categories such as books, manuscripts and artifacts. Some of these collections constitute materials which are, for example, generally considered by the Historical Manuscripts Commission on account of their form, or by the Museum Documentation Association because of their location. However, there is a vast quantity of non-book printed material which falls under none of these jurisdictions and of which there is no centralised record or list.

Such collections may be held in private hands or in institutions whose main purpose is not information gathering, such as industrial concerns or governmental agencies. They are also to be found within institutions which have a custodial function, like archives, museums and libraries. The location of such materials in any particular place does not define their form or content, nor does it say anything about how well they are organised or how accessible they are to outsiders.

Collections can be said to exist in three basic forms. Firstly they can be 'dead', that is already delineated, reduced to order, and possibly even listed. Such collections can have a sacrosanct 'archival' order, or else be organised according to their own particular logic or history. Secondly, there are 'formed' collections which may already be organised or even partially listed, but are still growing or being rearranged. The third form of collections consists of the working papers of individuals or organisations. These are often only intended for short-term use, and are constantly being added to or extracted from. They usually disappear, but are nearly always the starting point for the collections in the first and second categories.

Beyond the collections

What is the best way to make it possible to find out about collections of paper and associated materials that fall into the categories outlined? Can they or should they be looked at in the same way?

There are few useful purposes served by approaching the many varieties of collections considered in this research from the point of view of their form rather than their content. Thus 'ephemera collections' such as those considered in Chapter Two can be studied from the point of view of printing techniques or to 'get the feel of a period'. Nevertheless even they need to be broken down into ad hoc subject divisions, since this is the only practical means of entry into them.

One of the greatest difficulties besetting the resolution of the problems posed in this research has been the minefield of differences of definition and jurisdiction. Many of these have been outlined. Little serious purpose can be served by creating more sub-divisions within this field, such as between 'ephemera', 'minor publications', or 'reports', or between 'dead' and 'live' collections. Though it might be possible to consider different means of approach for such separate groups of material, the boundaries are always so indistinct that to try to define them precisely would simply be to create new problems. It is both necessary and possible to propose a unified form of approach to non-book printed materials, whose source, character and setting may vary a great deal.

There will be no Utopia where all the printed paper that there is in Britain (let alone the entire world), and all that is currently being produced, could be collected. Nor can there ever be a happy land where every item will one day be recorded, complete with cross-references to every conceivable means of finding it. This is not to say that there are not always ways in which books, other printed materials or artifacts might not be better collected or recorded. Clearly it is always possible to improve upon the estimable efforts of the Copyright Libraries, the British National Bibliography, the National Register of Archives, and other such institutions. There exists nevertheless a large lacuna in access to large amounts of printed material of widespread interest, which could be filled without overwhelming effort on this side of Utopia.

If the information set out in these pages has shown one thing it is that there is no serious difficulty for an individual outsider to approach a new subject field, to move from staging post to staging post within the network of those inside its ambit, and very rapidly to produce a wider range of knowledge of sources of information than any one individual already there. Such a project carried on continually in the form of a centrally organised account of collections could easily and inexpensively add to the sum of human knowledge. It would be widely welcomed and used.

Therefore, the best solution to the problem posed at the beginning of this research would be to establish a National Register of Collections, located within the Reference Division of the British Library. It is not difficult to set out how such a register would work, to outline its value to the community of learning, and to explain the reason for putting forward its particular form and location.

Some points on history

Before describing the National Register of Collections, it is necessary to say a word on the evolution of discussion on this matter, which, to say the least, has been protracted. Pemberton's 1971 Report has already been referred to a number of times.(7) Its main proposal for a National Documents Library did not win wide-spread support, partly on the grounds that the functions envisaged by such an agency could just as easily be performed by extending the resources and functions of the Copyright Receipt Office, the Copyright Agency and the British National Bibliography. However, as was emphasised in the introductory chapter, less emphasis in discussion on the Pemberton Report has been placed on his view that before anything else could be done, a national register of collections would need to be set up. This was considered at two conferences run by Aslib Social Sciences Group after Pemberton's report came out, and a number of discussions have taken place, particularly within the British Library Reference Division, since that time. The main conclusion of the Reference Division discussions was that they should take over the running of a national register of collections. However, the value of these conclusions was impaired by their concentration on the particular development of the BL, and the limited information about collections outside the BL system.

The present work was initiated in part as an attempt to remedy those deficiencies. There has already been an explanation of why its approach to the problem of non-book printed materials has been through the collections themselves. The survey has been undertaken by a researcher who is also quite outside the world of librarianship, with its own particular intrigues and passions. It is necessary to emphasise therefore that the conclusions arrived at from this very different approach, and without any partisan prejudice or predilection, are very close to those from within the Reference Division itself. Nor are there serious differences at least with the starting point put forward by Pemberton. What follows is an outline of some of the details of how a National Register of Collections would work. It is not quite the same as the ideas previously put forward and, because of the research on which it is based, is able to be more detailed in certain particulars and to approach certain of the problems somewhat differently. However, it is in all important respects the same idea first floated by Pemberton and argued in more detail in 1975 by a Reference Division Working Party. After almost a decade it is even more urgent that this idea should be made flesh.

How the National Register of Collections would work

The NRC would compile lists of collections of non-book printed materials in accession order. These would be most easily put together in the same form of flexible bindings that are used at the National Register of Archives. The list would be built best by concentrating on individual subjects as has been done in this Report, or else by working in particular local areas.

The definition of the term 'collection' would need to be as broad as possible so as to include, for example, individuals and private collectors where possible, and clubs and pressure groups within individual fields. This would of necessity include institutions whose existence was somewhat feeble or fleeting. An important detail in every entry would be on the level of accessibility of the collection.

There can be no standard way in which the NRC would work, for example by means of a particular form of postal survey. If it may be suggested, a combination of visits, telephone calls, letters and all other forms of communication that were used in this survey, would provide the most practical means of gathering together the necessary information.

The Register would first process its accession lists by producing a subject based index on the same lines as the National Register of Archives, going to as comprehensive a level as demand for its services indicate and as resources will allow. This would attempt to develop a system of cross-references whose detail and form would be subject to similar constraints. For example, it could encourage and work with the amateurs already in the field to find important but isolated postal history items over a wide range of various types of collections. Such a record could initially be kept on cards, but could easily be transferred to an on-line computer retrieval system by any of the well-known methods.

The Register would process this information by producing lists of collections in various fields, again according to demand and resources.

These could be produced in the form of occasional publications of the NRC, though might be even more useful in the trade press of the subjects under consideration. For at least two of the three topics considered in this research, such surveys could now be published and the very process of doing so would no doubt throw up further information.

Although the NRC would always aim to make its lists as comprehensive as possible, clearly the information available on collections would vary from very general descriptions to a detailed account of each item. The Register would encourage more detailed cataloguing within individual collections, and would discuss simplified and standardised means of going about this in the same way as the Museum Documentation Association does within its particular sphere. It would also discuss with those holding similar ranges of materials how these could be organised in a compatible way, if not pooled. It is possible to give an example of how this might work. A number of national pressure groups in the housing field hold collections of similar materials, somewhat variably organised. Those who hold them are largely unaware of what is held elsewhere. There would be no great labour in working out a standard series of headings which would allow outsiders and insiders to scan the different collections for their particular strong points or the special items they contain.

Although not in itself a custodial body, the NRC would aim at the preservation and improved organisation of information by directing those who hold collections to others in the field or to relevant material or to local custodial institutions. It has not been difficult during the course of this research to find cases of lack of contact between those holding similar collections within different institutional networks, be they libraries, museums or local government departments. This role of the NRC in bringing individuals and networks into contact with one another would, for example, allow ways to be found of preserving materials collected by short-lived pressure groups or by quangos cut down in their prime. The holders of at least one large collection encountered in this research, containing many millions of items and almost a household world in some circles, are worried about the ultimate fate of the material under their charge. At this point they have no idea where to turn in dealing with it.

Another side to the work of the NRC would be the encouragement of local bibliographies, both of currently produced materials and of those already in collections. This could be done partly through the somewhat patchy voluntary efforts now being made in this direction in certain parts of the country, and partly through what is already being done in the public library and archive system. The approach dictated by the brief of this particular research has given less emphasis to this local 'horizontal' way into the problems it considers than it merits. However, the 'Investigation of Local Minor Publications' of Diana Dixon and Paul Sturges at Loughborough University has made various suggestions in this direction.(8) The value of a National Register would be in the standardisation of various approaches in different parts of the country not adequately catered for by local effort.

In order to explain the conclusion that has been arrived at about the location of a National Register it is necessary to consider some possible alternatives:

1 It has been maintained that perhaps the functions envisaged for the NRC could be carried out federally by government departments, learned societies and so forth. There are numerous arguments against this. It would restrict the linking of collections, and would be more distant from the 'anti-establishment' parts of any network. It would also serve to create a new set of boundaries that would simply complicate the problems.

2 It has also been argued that the best approach to the problem would be through various local and specialist agencies, particularly as much ephemera is only of limited interest or application. However, without a national network of some sort it would be more difficult to standardise and improve methods of organisation, and to resolve precisely the biggest problem of all, which is to devise means of entry to material other than those which arise accidentally from the ways they are published or arranged. After 'I sprang to the stirrups', it took a great deal of energy and no little time 'to bring the good news from Ghent to Aix'.(9) Yet it took a good deal longer with more sophisticated forms of transporting information for the news about a report on caravaning published by the local authority in Scarborough to get as far as Leeds, although it contains a great deal more than local interest. Nor has the report, as far as can be discovered, yet found its way into any national housing bibliography or information network.(10) There is much information locally generated and difficult to find which nevertheless has no special significance in its area of origin. The most quoted example of this is in the reports of research produced in university departments.

3 It might also be argued that the NRC could be located within one of the national institutions that covers part of the field. One might mention, simply by way of example, the Library Association, Aslib and the Historical Manuscripts Commission. However, these institutions have special functions to perform in their own fields, in serving public libraries, specialist libraries and archival bodies. This would tend to limit their effectiveness for the sort of work outlined here.

4 It has also been argued that a new independent institution should be set up as the National Register of Collections, along the lines of the

Historical Manuscript Commission and its NRA. The argument against this course of action is not simply that it would probably be more costly than all the possible alternatives. Any new agency would have the additional and gratuitous problem of having to make itself known to a wide range of organisations and individuals, not simply in the worlds of learning, librarianship and the like.

Beyond these arguments against the alternatives, there are certain positive advantages in placing the NRC within the British Library, where it would seem to fit most logically into the Reference Division. For one thing, a good deal of work in locating and identifying collections would in any case have to take place within the BL itself. An agency located there could more easily work closely, as it would have to, with the Bibliographical Services Division and Copyright Receipt Office, as well as such outside bodies as the National Register of Archives and the Museum Documentation Association. Though not necessarily renowned for this particular line of business, the BL Reference Division is more widely known than most alternatives, and could more easily develop the supply and demand for the functions of the NRC. Though it is clearly not possible to completely resolve this particular problem, the BL on the whole is regarded with less suspicion by 'anti-establishment' bodies than are government departments and semi-governmental agencies. The more difficult and marginal organisations outside the mainstream could more easily be persuaded to cooperate with an institution working under the auspices of a body that there are some grounds for considering to have an independence from the State authorities and the present order of things.

Functions of the NRC

There are at least two arguments against the NRC which can be used to indicate the strengths of such an institution and the functions it would be able to perform.

The most obvious argument against the NRC is that it would be an expensive new state-assisted enterprise at a time of demolition rather than construction of such things. Yet this book has clearly shown that for a very limited outlay, it would be possible to materially improve the work of the BNB and locally based efforts along the same lines. From within the British Library it would be possible not simply to explore new territories in the world of collections but to sail further into many parts of the unchartered seas beyond those in which the copyright enforcement agencies operate in practice. At more than one point in this research, items were turned up which 'would have been' in BNB, or 'might have gone' to the Reports Collection of the Lending Division. A new agency with the functions of the NRC would directly service these and other parts of the library system. Through 'contacts' and

92

'networks' it could get a great deal of its work done by the amateurs and professionals in particular fields, in the same way as does the NRA and MDA. It is also possible to conceive of the National Register of Collections paying its way through the carrying out of 'contract work' for those in particular fields of interest.

The second major argument against the NRC is that it would not be used because the 'networks' within the various subject areas already allow enough access to the information it would contain. This book has demonstrated that while an independent researcher in very diverse subject areas can get into a 'network' and around it, those at any one point within it do not necessarily know what else there is, or how to go about finding out about it. No useful purpose could have been served in this book by giving examples of the experts who said 'go here and you will discover such and such', when there was nothing to be found there, or no such thing. Yet many such stories could have been told. Such events occur in all research of course, but it would not be difficult to reduce their incidence by means of the NRC. This does not mean it is easy to 'prove' to what extent any new referral agency would be used. There will of course always be those in this imperfect world who cannot or will not utilise the resources that are available, or do not get to know about them. The only means in any way scientific that it has been possible to use while compiling this book has been simply to ask people what they thought of a National Register of Collections. On the whole the actual practitioners in the fields themselves were less enthusiastic than those responsible for collecting and retrieving information. A librarian at the end of a long line within the housing network went so far as to say that a national register, 'which would list (reports) and make lists of documents in specific subject fields available would make life easier for us all, not to mention a national documents library'. It is at this 'secondary level', as a referral agency for professionals—including those in the record offices, the resource centres, the public libraries and the specialist libraries—that the NRC could be and would be a boon to all. Even if an individual enquiry did not start there, it could be directed there. At the NRC a very small group of people with their lists and their indexes, with their contacts and their occasional publications, could easily be in a position to provide access to information available in no other way, to improve the operations of those working near its own concerns, and to move one small necessary step towards a world where printed paper can be better stored, recorded and retrieved.

NOTES TO CHAPTER NINE

1 The nearest thing to such a figure that could be found is in the *Business monitor* of the Business Statistics Office, published by HMSO in August 1979 (reference PQ 489) and covering general printing and

publishing. Here the value of books produced by enterprises above 25 employees in 1978 is given as £510,025,000. The value of all other published matter produced by similar enterprises including greetings cards, diaries and so forth is £170,852,000. A further figure of sales of time-tables, calendars, admission tickets, packaging and much else is £168,582,000. To determine actual quantities of the products themselves does not appear possible, though there are some well-known figures for books, and for newspaper production.

2 Records Management Groups of the Society of Archivists *Records management* 1977, 36-7 on the proceedings of a conference shows very clearly that variation of views between public archivists and private records managers can derive from very different views about the stuff they are actually dealing with.

3 An excellent common sense example is to be found in the dividing lines used in the British Library's *Eighteenth century short title catalogue*, though some problems arise from a determination to separate 'printed' from 'manuscript' items. See Alston, R C and Jannetta, M J *Bibliography, machine-readable catalogue and the ESTC* 1978 17-18.

4 Cook, M *Archives administration. A manual for intermediate and smaller organisations and for local government* 1977 119-20.

5 Walker, G 'Planning, compiling and co-ordinating guides to resources' *Humanities information research: proceedings of a seminar. Sheffield 1980* edited by Sue Stone and published by the Centre for Research in User Studies, University of Sheffield, BL R&D Report 5588, 61-8 reflects this attitude. See also his 'Describing and evaluating library collections' *Journal of librarianship* October 1978.

6 There are some pertinent remarks on the necessity to break away from the rigid techniques of librarianship in Turner, M L 'Printed ephemera', an unpublished paper delivered to the Double Crown Club on 22nd January, 1980.

7 Pemberton, J E *The national provision of printed ephemera in the Social Sciences* University of Warwick, 1971.

8 Sturges, R P and Dixon, D *An investigation of local publications* BL R&D Report, May 1980.

9 Browning, Robert 'How they brought the good news from Ghent to Aix' in *Poems* 1909 edition, 3.

10 Scarborough Borough Council *Accommodating the caravan* Scarborough, 1975.

APPENDIX ONE

GENERAL EPHEMERA COLLECTIONS AND SOURCES

1 *John Johnson Collection, Bodleian Library, Oxford, OX1 3BG*
The many millions of separate items are described and illustrated in the
sources given in Chapter Two, Notes 1, 2, 6 and 7. More detailed
descriptions of parts of the collection are in Feather, J P *Book prospectuses before 1801 in the John Johnson Collection* Oxford, 1976,
Tonkin, J 'Theatre material in the John Johnson Collection' *Theatre
notebook* 26 1971-2 and Otley, G *Railway history. A guide* Leicester,
1973, 20-4. There is a duplicated list of *Main subject headings* August
1979, 11 pp, which provides the means of entry into boxes and folders
arranged entirely by their subject matter. Within the headings there is
as much detail as seems appropriate, and a logic of internal arrangement
following no systematic scheme. Thus, material from publishers is
arranged alphabetically by names, and postcards, cigarette cards, or
book plates according to their own particular systems. Entry is sometimes through the form of material, but generally through subject
headings supplemented by more detailed lists which can in principle
be expanded.

2 *Printers files in the National Library of Wales, Aberystwyth, Dyfed
SY23 3BU*
Two printers files, one from the office of I. and M. Thomas of Cardigan,
giving items printed there and described in Ballenger's book (see Chapter
Two, Note 3). The other is from J. T. Jones of Aberdare including
items printed by himself and some other printers.

3 *The Soulby Collection, Barrow-in-Furness Library, Ramsden Square,
Barrow-in-Furnace, Cumbria, LA14 1LL*
679 items from John Soulby the elder and other printers, 1796 to 1827,
arranged broadly by place and/or subject.

4 *Institute of Agricultural History and English Museum of Rural Life,
University of Reading, Whiteknights, Reading RG6 2AG*
Has 497 similar items printed by the younger John Soulby from 1821
to 1827, and a few items from other Northern printers, as well as a
late nineteenth century collection, from a jobbing printer called William

Kitchen and his son, described in a 1974 booklet, *The Kitchen collection.*

5 *Printing specimen books of Messrs Jennings and Bewley of Ware in Hertfordshire Record Office, County Hall, Hertford, SG13 8DE*
Six volumes cover 1918-20, at D/ES275, much local material—everything from dealers in old clothes to the Hertfordshire Historical Association. Mostly pasted in albums and not in a very good state of repair.

6 *Robert Wood Collection, Hartlepool Museum, Clarence Road, Hartlepool, Cleveland, TS24 8BT*
Accounts can be found in note 5 of Chapter Two. About 50,000 items are arranged in boxes and envelopes according to a general system of headings along the same lines as John Johnson. This is a list of the main headings: Agriculture (2 boxes); Auctions (7); Coal (2); Coronations and Jubilees 1838-1935 (8 envelopes); Docks and Harbours (7 boxes); Education (8 boxes); Elections (2 boxes on local Hartlepool, 1 on South Durham Parliamentary, 1 on Hartlepool Parliamentary, 1 on Hartlepool Municipal Council); Entertainment (3 boxes); Finance and Commerce (4, including banks and property for sale); Free Trade (4 envelopes); Health and Hospitals (2 boxes); Hotels and Catering (2); Insurance (2); Iron and Steel (2); Law and Order (4); Manuscripts (12 boxes arranged mainly under subject headings); Military Testimonials (1); Newspapers (various isolated local copies 1866-1970); Printing and Publishing (2 boxes); Religion (13 boxes by religious groups); Road and Rail Transport (1); Shops (about 14 boxes, by trades and alphabetically within them); Shipping (about 18 boxes mostly arranged by topics like shipowners' firms, pay and conditions etc.); Shipbuilding (9 boxes); Social Stationery (5 boxes of visiting cards, morning cards etc.); Societies (7 boxes and 11 envelopes); Sports (about 8 boxes); Tailors, Miliners etc. (4 boxes and one envelope); Temperance (2 boxes, 2 envelopes); Trade and Industry (about 8 boxes including tradesmen, shops etc.); Transport (4); Trips and Excursions (4).

7 *The Ephemera Society, 12 Fitzroy Square, London, W1P 5HQ*
Issues a magazine, organises sales and lectures, of special interest to collectors.

8 *National Library of Scotland, George IV Bridge, Edinburgh, EH1 1EW*
Collections include Scottish political ephemera.

9 *Modern Records Centre, University of Warwick Library, Coventry CV4 7AL*
Includes much material of general interest to economic and social historians in its various collections.

10 *Department of Prints and Drawings, Guildhall Library, Aldermanbury, London EC2P 2EJ*
Includes many collections of 'pure ephemera' largely of cultural interest. Examples include the Phillips Collection of about 800 packs of playing cards, the Knaser Collection of Stationer's Labels Trade Card Collection

(c 1,500 items from 1750 to 1850), Playbills and Theatre Programmes Collection (about 15000 items, mostly from 1700-1900) Book-plate Collection (2,333 items), Civic Entertainments Collection (1727-date). Some of the 'artificial' collections contain much ephemera—eg the vast Noble Collection of London typography and The Phillip Norman scrapbooks of London inns and taverns. Much of this material is arranged chronologically or by place, but a few of the collections also have their own separate indexes.

11 *Ephemera Collection, Museum of London, 150 London Wall, London EC2Y 5HN*
Contains perhaps 1700 separate items arranged under such headings as Bills, Cards (calling), Cartoons, Cigarette Cards (about 150), Invitations, Postcards. The largest group is about 200 programmes.

12 *Tolson Memorial Museum, Ravensknowle Park, Huddersfield HD5 8DJ*
Has a small ephemera collection including advertising, bookmarks, theatre bills and programmes, political satires etc.

13 *The Country Life Archive, National Museum of Antiquities of Scotland, Queen Street, Edinburgh, EH2 1SD*
Includes much of general material on such matters as housing, transport and so forth under 29 general headings and numerous sub-headings.

14 *British Library Reference Division, Great Russell Street, London WC1B 3DG*
See Chapter Two p26 for a discussion of how to find relevant material.

15 *Shoe and Shoemaking Documents and Ephemera, Shoe Museum, Central Museum, Guildhall Road, Northampton NN1 1DP*
Headings are Northamptonshire shoemakers, Education, Apprenticeship Indentures, the Union, British Boot and Shoe Institutions, Foremen's Associations, Non-Northampton Shoemakers, Miscellaneous, Boot and Shoe Price Lists, Catalogues, Designs, Accounts, Advertisements, Posters, Leather.

16 *The Theatre Museum, Victoria and Albert Museum, London, SW7 2RL*
Includes over 200,000 playbills, together with programmes, posters, music sheets and much else being brought together from a number of collectors, of which the most well-known is the one donated by Gabrielle Enthoven in 1925. Access to this material is currently limited until its removal to a special site in Covent Garden in 1983.

17 *Local History Library, Central Library, Newcastle on Tyne NE99 1MC*
Contains some volumes of broadsides from 1751 to 1861 at L020 as well as albums of newspaper cuttings. Also L324 has a fair amount of ephemeral electoral literature, mainly from the 1790s to the 1880s. More recent posters, programmes, handbills and so forth are recorded on cards and bound in volumes.

18 *Cambridgeshire Collection, Central Library, 7 Lion Yard, Cambridge CB2 3NA*

Includes scrapbooks and hand bills from the mid-nineteenth century, numerous photographs and sale catalogues arranged by place, and more modern material arranged under organisations, firms, clubs and so forth. Other material is placed in boxes by the year.

19 *Cambridge Papers, University Library, West Road, Cambridge CB3 9DR*

These documents, consisting predominantly of ephemeral printed material and sometimes known as the Cam Collection began with the combination of a number of sets of nineteenth century papers reflecting all aspects of life in the University. It has since been supplemented and systematically arranged there now being a vigorous acquisition policy amongst likely sources of supply. The library published in 1939 a *Cambridge Papers Classification* which divides the collection into A Administrative, B Finance, C Legislation, D Studies, E Teaching Officers Lectures Examinations, F Buildings and Institutions, G Scholarships and Prizes, H Degrees, I University Representation, J University Societies, M Miscellaneous.

20 *The Library of Contemporary Cultural Records, English Faculty Library, Sidgewich Avenue, Cambridge CB3 9DA*

The collection aims to provide 'material for an outline picture of the cultural situation in Britain at the present time', including 'popular' culture. The material is divided into the following sections: General, Fine and Applied Arts, Music, Theatre and Film, Literary Activity, Adult Studies, Libraries, Museums and Local Archives, Publishing and Bookselling, Radio and Television and various smaller groups such as 'pop' festivals and tourism. A full description of the conception behind the library is to be found in *Times Literary Supplement* March 3, 1972. It may soon move to some other location outside Cambridge.

APPENDIX TWO

COLLECTIONS INCLUDING POSTAL HISTORY

1 *Post Office Records, Postal Headquarters, St Martin's-Le-Grand, London EC1A 1LP*
The material, which is more generally described in Chapter Three is divided into a series of classifications from Post 1 to Post 100 (some of the numbers as yet unused). Post 1 contains Treasury letter books from 1688 to 1931. Post 2-9 are various sets of financial accounts from 1677 to 1953. Post 10-28 contains sets of minutes and files on inland mails, for example Post 17 deals with the organisation of circulating and sorting from 1797 to 1954. Post 29-38 contains various sets of minutes dealing with the packet service, Ireland, Scotland and so forth. Post 35 is 1,708 volumes of the Postmaster General's minutes from 1744 to 1920. These are all indexed. Post 39-42 has a series of reports up to the mid-nineteenth century. Post 43-51 deals with the various aspects of overseas mail services. Post 53 covers postage rates and Post 54 stamps. Post 57 and 60-66 deals with various aspects of the staff from 1766 to 1956. Post 67 deals with letters patent 1715-1915 and Post 68 has 570 volumes of rules and instructions from 1729 to 1952. Post 70 deals with the Advisory Council which existed from 1921 to 1963. Post 74-9 covers various Post Office departments: savings, supplies and so forth. Post 81-8 covers telecommunications. Post 91 is buildings. Post 94 onwards are largely sets of private papers of various Postmasters General and Secretaries. Post 100 includes some of the papers of Rowland Hill for 1836 to 1879 of which there is a separate detailed list. There is a similar list for Lord Walsingham 1787-1794. There are drawers of cards giving some cross-references by subject.
2 *Postal History Collection, Bruce Castle Museum, Lordship Lane, London N17 8NU*
This contains about 20,000 individual items divided by the same system into a number of groups of types of material described in Chapter Three. Details are given in note 5 of Chapter Three of published accounts of the collection. It is divided by a numerical system as follows. 000-090 is Miscellaneous including relevant theatre programmes,

verse, the Post Office in wartime. 100-190 is General History divided chronologically. 200-290 is Organisation of the Postal Services, 210 for example dealing with the Postmaster General, 250 with the London Postal Service. 200-390 is Post Office Staff, 330 being Postmen, 360 Women Employees. 400 is Finance, in which is incorporated from 460 methods of collecting postage including stamps, then further sub-divided. 500-590 deals with the collection, distribution and delivery of mails, 510 being Inland, 560 Foreign and Colonial. 600-690 is communications in general including roads, railways. 700-790 covers various forms of telecommunications. 800-890 covers minor services such as 870 Money Orders. 900-90 deals with non-British Post Offices, sub-divided by country. Besides the material being arranged in this way, there is an accessions catalogue on individual cards covering the last ten years.

3 *The National Postal Museum, King Edward Street, London EC1A 1LP.*
Includes the Phillips Collection, nearly all stamps, but covers everything from the 1830s reform movements to 1901 in the British postal system and the correspondence books of the De La Rue Company which printed stamps and banknotes.

4 *The Royal Philatelic Collection, Buckingham Palace, London SW1A 1AA*
Details in the book cited in note 6 of Chapter Three.

5 *The Library, National Philatelic Society, 1 Whitehall Place, London SW1A 2HE*
Has some books on local studies, guides and periodicals.

6 *The Library, Royal Philatelic Society, 41 Devonshire Place, London W1N 1PE*
Not open to non-members.

7 *Bath Postal Museum, 51 Great Pulteney Street, Bath BA2 4DP*
Opened on 28 April 1979. Has begun to accumulate material, some on short-term loan, not yet listed.

8 *British Library Philatelic Collection, Great Russell Street, London WC1 3DG*
Includes, besides Tapling and other stamp collections, collections of Inland Revenue Archives, Air Post material, Speswick Collection of Postal Stationary of the World.

9 *British Library Reference Division, Great Russell Street, London WC1 3DG*
Relevant materials scattered throughout the Library. For example, BP3 is a collection of official returns and notices from 1756 to 1842 and BP 3/2 is eleven volumes of minutes, reports, newspaper cuttings and manuscripts. Miscellaneous 1882 C 2/3 is a volume of items including a pamphlet on John Chalmers' claim to have invented the penny post and a leaflet from the 1849 campaign against Sunday labour

in the Post Office. BS 31/28 contains Post Office posters from the First World War. BS 31/138 contains a large collection of leaflets and other ephemera dealing with recruitment, uniforms and much else. BS 68/166 contains nearly 100 separate items on the Post Office Giro. Some, but by no means all, of this can be found under the heading England-Post Office, in the Catalogue though only described in the most general terms.

10 *John Johnson Collection, Bodleian Library, Oxford OX1 3BG*
Includes F. A. Bellamy Collection which is mostly philatelic but has other relevant items also.

11 *National Maritime Museum, Greenwich, London SE10 9NF*
Has the Frank Staff Collection of Sea Mail Covers arranged in 36 cabinets chronologically and by shipping lines.

12 *The Castle Museum, Norwich NR1 3JU*
Collection of postmarks stored alphabetically in files. Active policy of collecting Norfolk postal history details of which are on a card index.

13 *Aeronautics Department, Science Museum, London SW7 5NH*
The collection of Miss W. Penn-Gaskell, acquired in 1948, contains covers, pictures and much else on the history of air postage. Each item is mounted and described and there are separate indexes of the pictures.

14 *Tolson Memorial Museum, Ravensknowle Park, Wakefield Road, Huddersfield HD5 8DJ*
Has the Frank Buckley collection of postmarks covering parts of Yorkshire for 1744 to 1850 (25 postmarks).

15 *The Library of the Victoria and Albert Museum, South Kensington, London SW7 2RL*
Has two albums of documents relating to the founding of the penny post including proofs of stamps and registered letters compiled by Sir Henry Cole.

16 *Modern Records Centre in the Library of the University of Warwick, CV4 7AL*
Has most of the historical records of the Post Office Engineering Union and of other important organisations like the Post Office Whitley Council Staff Side. It also has a small amount from the Union of Communication Workers and some of its breakaway organisations.

17 *Research Department, Union of Communication Workers, Crescent Lane, London SW4 9RN*
Has some relevant material under its own system of numerical headings. 100-139 is Postal Workers' Organisations, 200-299 is Post Office Workers, 300-399 is Post Office Conditions, 500-599 is Post Office Administration, 600 is International from labour and Post Office viewpoints.

18 *House of Lords Record Office, London SW1A OPW*
Has two albums of envelopes addressed or franked by peers. Other relevant materials amongst private collections of papers are not separately indexed.

19 *The County Archives, Hertford County Record Office, County Hall, Hertford SG13 3DE*
At D/E X26 is the Graveson Collection which consists predominately of covers, postmarks etc from or to Hertfordshire from 1750 to 1880 illustrating various local offices, early stamps etc. There is also some little correspondence with the secretary of the Post Office and other relevant papers. The Edward Hall letters at D/25 illustrate various phases of the local postal system from c1880 to the 1930s. The old subject card index allows other items to be identified such as the Berkhampstead Post Office in 1890 at D/E Bu B 38. However, the methods of listing employed since 1962 do not allow items dealt with since that date to be separately identified in this way.

20 *Surrey Record Office, County Hall, Penrhyn Road, Kingston upon Thames, Surrey KT1 2DN*
More typically, the subject index here allows the location of a dozen or so individual items of postal interest.

21 *The Suffolk Record Office, County Hall, Ipswich ID4 2JS*
Has little separate postal history material besides a full file of the East Anglia Postal History Circle Bulletin from 1962.

22 *Staffordshire County Record Office, County Buildings, Eastgate Street, Stafford ST16 2LZ*
Includes in the Dartmouth Papers (at DCW 1778/11/20) a volume containing an account of the work of the Post Office in June 1677.

23 *Derbyshire County Record Office, County Offices, Matlock, Derbyshire DE4 3AG*
Besides an NRA Reference to a collection of envelopes with postmarks for 1831-9 in the Rodes of Barlborough family papers, there is also a list which has been compiled of items of postal interest from the 1670s to 1800 in the papers of Okeover, Fitzherbert and Gall.

24 *Leeds Public Library Reference Department, Central Library, Leeds LS1 3AB*
Has a Collection of Cancellations from Yorkshire towns arranged in alphabetical order, some pre-twentieth century from the Leeds Philatelic Society. A similar collection for Leeds of 38 covers and two maps encompasses all the forms of postage from 1782 to 1855. There is also a collection of stamps, postmarks and covers relating to Yorkshire from the nineteenth century and brought together by F. Buckley. A similar collection by Edwin Peters deals with Horsforth from 1822 to 1963.

25 *The Archives Department, Central Library, St Peter's Square, Manchester M2 5PD*

The Charles Roeder Collection (M277) contains at 10/8 to 10/11 various relevant items including large numbers of eighteenth century postmarks. A list of relevant items from other collections covers 1784 to 1937, some items not simply of local interest.

26 *Archives Department, Halifax Central Library, Lister Lane, Halifax, Calderdale HX1 5LA*

Has papers on the Halifax to Ripperden Gig Mail of 1835-6 in the Field House Estate papers at FH:393.

27 *Local Collection, Uxbridge Library, 22 High Street, Uxbridge, London Borough of Hillingdon UB8 1HD*

Bound volume of Uxbridge postmarks 1765-1951 collected by Mr W. Milligan. The local studies librarian is also able to provide some published articles and photographs.

28 *The Postal History Society*

This body which caters for all interests in the field was founded in 1936. The current Secretary is Mr J. G. S. Scott of 5 Bayswater Street, London SW3 4XD. It produces the bi-monthly *Postal history* and various occasional publications. The President of the Society, Mr R. M. Willcocks of 7 Shooters Hill Road, London SE3 7AR, is the doyen of the field and has produced the most detailed reference works.

29 *Great Britain Postal History Group*

This is part of the PHS catering for this specialism. The Secretary is Mr A. J. Kirk of 123 Benhill Road, London SE5 7LZ, and the Editor of its magazine *The British mailcoach* Mr M. V. D. Champness of The Old Vicarage, Wendens Ambo, Saffron Waldon, Essex CB11 4JY has a comprehensive knowledge and interest in the field.

30 *The Society of Postal Historians*

This is a body to which those who have shown particular achievements in the field are elected. The Secretary is Mr R. I. Johnson of 65 Manor Park, Bristol BS 7HW and the Editor of their publications is Mr Dennis Vanderveldte of 25 Sinclair Grove, London NW11 9JH, who takes a special interest, inter alia, in disinfected letters.

31 *London Postal History Group*

Secretary is Rev A. J. Potter of St Hugh's, Old Hall Green, Ware, Hertfordshire SE11 1DR. They are in the process of producing a very detailed 'Handbook' in sections.

32 *Yorkshire Postal History Society*

Set up in 1957, the Secretary is Mr W. A. Sedgewick, 25 Hunters Lane, Sheffield S13 8LA. This Society has published over a dozen local histories and some other works. The Secretary says that besides items 14 and 24 above, the best public collections in the country which can be used for postal history purposes are in the Sheffield County Library, The Wilberforce Museum, High Street, Hull, Temple Newsome Archives Leeds, York Central Library, Keighley Library and Halifax Museum.

Further examples are given in publications of the Society, of which one of the best is M. T. Groves and J. A. Fowler *Postal History of Kingston-upon-Hull, Hebden and Holderness* 1974.

33 *The Midland (GB) Postal History Society*

The Secretary, Mr W. S. Chester of 17 Rock Close, Coventry CV6 7HG, himself has a collection dealing with Coventry since 1741 which is open to inspection. Other members are prepared to respond to specific enquiries.

34 *The Postal History Society of Lancashire and Cheshire*

Founded in 1962, the Secretary is Mr Eric Hebden, 410 Rossendale Road, Burnley, Lancashire BB11 5HN.

35 *East Anglia Postal History Study Circle*

The Editor of the well-produced Bulletin is Ms Vivian Sussex of 21 Marshall Close, Sheering, Colchester, CO5 7LQ. Besides collection 21 above, postal historians in the area also use the Northampton and Cambridge Record Offices, and the archives of the Norwich Union Insurance at Surrey Street, Norwich.

36 *Somerset and Dorset Postal History Group*

The Secretary, Mr T. K. Brown, The Barn House, Chenton Hill, North Chenton, Templecombe, Somerset, is prepared to discuss collections with serious researchers. The Somerset Record Office is used by postal historians though it has no specific collections.

37 *Portsmouth and District Philatelic Society*

Lt Cdr C. A. Sinfield of 18 Chilgrove Road, Drayton, Portsmouth PO6 2ER, is Chairman of the Society and Curator of a postal history collection which can be used to answer individual enquiries by outsiders.

38 *Robson Lowe Limited, 60 Pall Mall, London SW17 5HZ*

Auction catalogues are available in the British Library and at the Bournemouth office at 39 Poole Hill.

39 *Harmers of London, 41 New Bond Street, London W1A 4EH*

This firm has recently begun to run specialised postal history sales, and the catalogue for the first of them, held on 21 February 1979, is widely available.

40 *Stanley Gibbons Auctions Ltd, Dusy House, Russell Street, London*

Also runs auctions of materials in this field.

APPENDIX THREE

SOME COLLECTIONS OF GREETINGS CARDS AND POSTCARDS

1 *The Library, Museum of London, 150 London Wall, London EC2Y 5HN*
The library has approximately 1900 Valentine Cards, a small part of the Jonathon King Collection. Some are still pasted into albums under rather general headings as King himself did them, but others have been mounted in boxes. Many, though by no means all, are recorded on a set of cards. The library also has an unsorted collection of Christmas cards and some picture postcards of the period 1900 to 1930.

2 *Print Room, Victoria and Albert Museum, London SW7 2RL*
At CG67 are three boxes containing about 580 Valentines, mostly described in considerable detail in the catalogue. At CG68 is a box of 485 Christmas, New Year, Easter and other greeting cards from 1875 to 1925, American, English and French. At 94E 14-19 there are cards of various types, trademen's cards, Valentine cards, Christmas cards and so forth, mostly donated in small collections.

3 *The Castle Museum, York YO1 1RY*
The Museum has in store a large collection of Valentine and other greetings cards, mostly donated by Dr Kirk in the 1940s. There is a small pamphlet describing them by Violet A. Wock entitled *A Chat on the Valentine Collection in the Castle Museum* York, 1949. Besides approximately 200 on exhibition, there are five boxes containing about 380 items, mostly Victorian Valentines, but also including various other greetings cards. There are two boxes of general greetings cards from the 1860s to the 1930s containing about 130 items; two boxes of about 150 Christmas cards from 1839 to 1970; a box of mourning cards (virtually all Victorian); a box with about 150 birthday cards, mostly early twentieth century and 1930s; a box containing about 50 miscellaneous cards, mostly birthday cards from about 1900, including some splendid cards with lace. The Museum also has a large collection of picture postcards which, besides covering Yorkshire typography also have pictures of libraries and art galleries, the First World War, people, sport, transport, royalty, holiday views etc. Some other Valentines

and such items can be found from the accession list, where they are described in considerable detail.

4 *British Library Reference Division, Great Russell Street, London WC1B 3DG*

Under the heading Valentine can be found a number of isolated items in collections, and pamphlets containing model verses.

5 *John Johnson Collection, Bodleian Library, Oxford OX1 3BG*

Has boxes of Valentine cards, boxes of other greetings cards which are not separately described. There are also postcards arranged under general subject headings.

6 *St Brides Printing Library, London EC4*

Has a small collection of Victorian Valentines.

7 *Shell Oil, Shell-Mex House, Strand, London WC2R ODX*

Has about 250 nineteenth and early twentieth century Valentines bought in 1964 from the 'Valentine Shop' of the Misses Samuels and now arranged in glass cases. Also has Valentines sent out by Shell from 1938 until the mid-60s.

APPENDIX FOUR

SUBJECT BASED REFERRAL AGENCIES

Some collections mentioned in Appendix One fulfil this role—No 4 for agriculture, No 15 for shoes, No 16 for theatre. Other gaps are filled by:

1 *The Group for Scientific Technological and Medical Collections c/o Ms Joan Smith of the Science Museum, London SW7 2DD*
This group of the Museum Association aims to discuss the problems of handling such materials including printed paper, in museums.

2 *The Contemporary Scientific Archives Centre, 20 Keble Road, Oxford OX1 3QC*
Catalogues and assists in the disposal of the papers of scientists who have died since 1945. Catalogues go to the National Register of Archives and elsewhere. For details see Margaret Gowing 'The Contemporary Scientific Archives Centre' *Notes and records of the Royal Society of London* 34, June 1979.

3 *The Contemporary Medical Archives Centre. Wellcome Institute of the History of Medicine, 183 Euston Road, London, NW1 2BP*
Aims to perform similar functions for medical papers.

APPENDIX FIVE

SOURCES FOR PICTURES OF DOMESTIC APPLIANCES

1 *Domestic Appliances Gallery, Science Museum, Exhibition Road, London SW7 5NH*
Artifacts from this section of the Museum are systematically photographed, mounted and kept on large card files. Ephemeral items including advertising and press cuttings are also collected, and there are a few dozen trade catalogues in the field. Some other relevant material is held in the gas and lighting departments.

2 *The Design Centre, 28 Haymarket, London SW1Y 4SU*
The Slide Library has under its Consumer Goods heading a number of relevant items, and also black and white pictures in what is known as its Archive with relevant items under the headings H (Heating) and K (Kitchen). The published Design Centre *Slide Library Catalogue* 1973 is soon to be replaced. There is also relevant material in holdings on the 1946 'Britain Can Make It' exhibition and the 1951 Festival of Britain. The Design Index contains some relevant pictures, though somewhat selective and all recent.

3 *Science Reference Library, The British Library, 9 Kean Street, London WC2B 4AT*
This annexe of the SRL contains manufacturers' catalogues, technical brochures, maintenance manuals, data and specification sheets, house journals, company newsletters, press releases, reprints of journal articles and annual reports. Much of this includes relevant material. As the subject index moves from the Patent Office Library system to a more comprehensive subject based organisation on microfiche, it will become increasingly possible to find material of the sort being sought in this survey. For a general description see M. J. Thomson 'Techno-commercial literature in the Science Reference Library' *ASLIB proceedings* May 28, 1976. There is a small amount of material on the shelves of the Holborn branch, formerly the Patent Office Library, at G5-G2 ('Electricity and electrical equipment') and GL-YM ('Gas').

4 *The Country Life Archive, National Museum of Antiquities of Scotland, Queen Street, Edinburgh EH2 1JD*

The archive contains cuttings and other relevant material in its section on The Home, as well as a few trade catalogues and a collection of photographs arranged by a system which has grown up with it. More details are in a duplicated *The country life archive—a short guide.*

5 *The Welsh Folk Museum, St Fagan's, Cardiff CF5 6XB*
A large collection of domestic artifacts are arranged under the general heading: Domestic Life—the Home: Domestic miscellania, housing, lighting. Photographs and slides of many of these items exist, arranged according to the same system.

6 *City of Portsmouth Museum, Museum Road, Old Portsmouth PO1 2LS*
The local history collection has some artifacts in the field, with a few relevant trade catalogues from around 1870.

7 *The Institute of Agricultrual History and Museum of English Rural Life, Whiteknights, The University, Reading RG6 2AG*
Some relevant material is to be found in the Photographs Collection under the headings 60 Domestic and 180 Lighting. The Institute places cuttings and similar material in a special category known as Classified Information. There is also a Documents Collection including isolated trade catalogues, with a series of archives of specific firms, mostly in agricultural engineering. Details of the arrangements are set out in various publications of the Institute on Museum Procedure: *Document collection* 1971, *Trade records* 1973 compiled by David Phillips, *Classification* 1978, *Photographs* 1978 compiled by Sadie B. Ward and *Library* 1978 by John S Creasey, the last using a quite separate system.

8 *The Scottish Record Office, The General Register House, Edinburgh EH1 3YY*
The C. Norman Kemp Muniments Collection (GD 327) contains some catalogues including material on lamps and other domestic appliances. There may be similar pictures in the Earl of Cromastie Muniments, but they are difficult to find because of lack of detail in the listings. There are some isolated trade catalogues in other collections.

9 *John Johnson Collection, Bodleian Library, Oxford OX1 3BG*
Contains relevant items under the headings Electricity, Oil Lamps, Fire Grates, Gas, Oil and Candles, Ironmongery, Sewing Cottons and Machines, and Electrical Appliances.

10 *BBC Hulton Picture Library, 35 Marylebone High Street, London W1M 4AA*
The subject headings that yielded most on this subject are Electricity, Gas, Home Life, Lighting, Heating, Ventialtion.

11 *The Mary Evans Picture Library, 1 Tranquil Vale, Blackheath, London SE3 OBU*
The Daily Life section under Cooking includes some pictures of utensils mostly extracted from magazines. The Household drawer has relevant

items under Appliances various, Cleaning Sweeping and Polishing, Decorating, Laundry, Home and Sewing Machines.

12 *The Mansell Collection, 42 Linden Gardens, London W2 4ER*
Has relevant material under the headings Food and Home Life.

13 *Institution of Gas Engineers, Panel for the History of the Industry, c/o Institution of Gas Engineers, 17 Grosvenor Crescent, London SW1 7ES*
The Panel has details of local holdings of artifacts and records as well as lists of those interested in them. The ultimate aim is to place individual items on a computerised data base. Though there is only a limited capacity to locate individual pictures at the moment, the procedure being developed should provide the best means for doing so.

14 *North Thames Gas Historical Collection at Redloh House, Fulham, London SW6*
The aim is eventually to set up a museum at a site to be decided, and at this stage the holdings (including paper) are only partly catalogued. Photographs and advertising material do not appear to have been retained in any systematic way by North Thames Gas. At this stage only serious and 'specific' enquiries can be answered.

15 *John Doran Museum, Aylestone Road, Leicester LE2 7QH*
Item 1316 is a 'Box containing various trade literature concerning domestic appliances', and this includes a number of catalogues and leaflets particularly from the 1930s and 50s. More generally, the well-organised and fully listed collection, for which a card index on a subject basis is being prepared, provides an essential tool for any serious student in this field.

16 *Scientific Information Centre, British Gas Corporation Research and Development Division, Watson House, Peterborough Road, London SW6 3HN*
The records of appliances which have been approved from 1930 are arranged according to a system of numbering by seven digits. The first digit is a main range of appliance—eg 1 is cooking appliances. The second digit covers type of appliance—12 is domestic cookers, including split level, built in, instant ignition. The next three digits cover the name of the manufacturer—032 is Abergas Ltd. The last two digits cover the model—01 is Leisure 60 Cooker. 11 264 is Domestic Cooker, Stoves, Cabaret 154. Page numbers are also given to British Gas *Manual of appliance identification. Domestic* 1975. This system provides by far the most systematic method of finding pictures of Household appliances discovered during the course of this research.

Watson House also has a large number of other pictorial items, including 10,000 slides of many items of which household appliances form a part. These are indexed by subject from 1967, and include cookers from the John Doran Museum along with other antique items.

There are also albums of photographs taken of an exhibition of historical gas appliances held as part of the Institution of Gas Engineers centenary celebrations in 1965.

On the work of the Watson House Research Station see E. A. K. Patrick *Watson House 1926-1976* 1976, which incidently contains photographs of most of the main developments in the design of household appliances.

Not all this material is necessarily publicly available.

17 *Electricity Council, 30 Millbank, London SW1P 4RD*

Holds much publicity and other material of which the most important for purposes of the present study are in the files of the Electrical Development Association (1919-65) including most of its (numbered) publications, largely advertising material. Typical examples are EDA publication 222 *The home of 1922*, a twelve page pamphlet giving pictures of all the appliances of that time, and 912 *Electricity plug points and their uses in the home* c1927 giving most appliances then in use. Most of the material is undated, but is arranged in approximately chronological order and could in principle be dated from internal evidence.

18 *Electrical Association for Women, 25 Foulbert's Place, London W1V 2AL*

Continually publishes relevant material.

19 *National Archive of Electrical Science and Technology, Institution of Electrical Engineers, Savoy Place, London WC2R OBL*

Most of the material here concerns the transmission of electricity rather than its application. However, there are pictures of most forms of electrical domestic appliances to be found in the Dame Caroline Haslett papers, particularly at NAEST 33/2.11.22 and the Report of the 12th Annual conference of the EAW at NAEST 33/2.11.5. The catalogue of the Women's First Electrical Exhibition (1946) at NA' 33/2.9 has pictures of every form of appliance then available, and at M340 E. Allen *Housing. A practical guide* 1953 contains pictures of various forms of irons. A typescript lecture by A. E. Jepson, a student at the Institute in 1905, entitled, *Electrical heating. Its history and development* includes slides of irons, saucepans, hotplates and heaters.

20 *The Milne Museum of Electricity, The Slade, Tonbridge, Kent TN9 1HR*

Includes a good number of trade catalogues and photographs, many still unsorted. For an account of the collection, see Chapter Five, note 19.

21 *The Electricity Council Museum Warehouse, Penrose Street, London SW17*

Includes a number of catalogues, scrapbooks, photographs, and other relevant material.

111

22 *Collection of Electrical Antiquities, East Midlands Electricity Board, Woodbridge Street, Nottingham*

Contains similar material—main details not available at the time this research was done because the material was being moved.

23 *Archives Department, John Lewis Partnership, Cavendish Road, Stevenage, Hertfordshire, SG1 2EH*

Illustrations in press cuttings and old catalogues would provide some pictures.

24 *Archives, Ferranti, Hollinwood, Lancashire OL9 JS*

Photographs and catalogues are available for 1910-18 and 1927-56 when the firm made domestic appliances. The professionally organised and listed archives of this company include under the companies that existed up to 1930 at Group 'B' B 5/19 on fires, cookers, waterheaters etc, 1913-15, and various other relevant documents. At B17/4.15 are photographs of domestic appliances for this period and at B19 publicity material on all electric homes of 1913-33. At C8/2. 16-20 there are papers from the radio and domestic appliance departments 1930-53, including miscellaneous leaflets from the latter. At C17/4.9 are photographs of radios, TVs etc 1935-57. At C17/4.17 are photographs of fires, waterheaters etc.

25 *The Customer Services Department, Hotpoint, Rye House, Hoddiston, Hertfordshire, EN11 OEL*

Can supply photographs of currently produced appliances.

26 *The Librarian, Hoover Ltd, Perivale, Greenford, Middlesex UB6 8DX*

The Public Affairs Department can supply photographs in response to specific enquiries.

27 *Belling Ltd, Bridge Works, Southbury Road, Enfield, Middlesex (PO Box 9, Enfield, Middlesex EN1 1UF)*

Though currently re-siting historical appliances, pictures from catalogues since 1912 can be supplied.

APPENDIX SIX

PICTURE COLLECTIONS AND RELEVANT ORGANISATIONS

1 *Courtauld Institute of Art, 20 Portman Square, London W1H 9HP*
2 *Social History Index, Scottish National Portrait Gallery, Queen Street, Edinburgh, EH2 1SD*
3 *BBC Hulton Picture Library, 35 Marylebone High Street, London W1M 4AA*
4 *The Mansell Collection, 42 London Gardens, London W2 4ER*
5 *The Mary Evans Picture Library, 1 Tranquil Vale, Blackheath, London SE3 OBU*
6 *Robert Harding Picture Library, 5 Boots Mews, Chepstow Road, London W2 5AG*
7 *Imperial War Museum, Lambeth Road, London SE1 6HZ*
8 *The Department of Prints and Drawings, Victoria and Albert Museum, Cromwell Road, London SW7 2RL*
9 *The Museum Documentation Advisory Unit, Imperial War Museum, Duxford, Cambridgeshire CB2 4QR*
10 *The Design History Society, c/o Mr R. G. Newport, 57 Greenhill, Blackwell, Bromsgrove, Worcestershire B60 1BL*

APPENDIX SEVEN

SOURCES FOR CURRENT HOUSING INFORMATION

1 *Library of the Department of the Environment, Marsham Street, London SW1P 3EB*
Besides the comprehensive library, and bibliographical service given in the text and in Chapter Seven note 1, it is worth mentioning that the library has development plans kept in boxes by the names of authorities and structure plans kept on shelves similarly organised. The relevant authorities have a legal obligation to supply them. There is also a separate pamphlet series arranged on the same basis as the main collection. Much more detail is given in the library's own publications —the most important for present purposes are listed in Chapter Seven, note 1, page 76 above.

2 *Distribution Unit, Building Research Establishment, Garston, Watford WD2 7JR*
Provides research and information about building techniques.

3 *Public Relations Department, The Housing Corporation, 149 Tottenham Court Road, London W1P OBN*
The Corporation issues an annual *Report* as well as a Programme full of details of the cooperative sector. Another important publication is *Co-ownership housing. What it is and where* 1979 which gives details of local schemes.

4 *The Housing Centre Trust, 62 Chandos Place, London WC2N 4HG*
On the general information providing functions of the Trust, see Chapter Seven and note 3. Amongst other things, the library has a miscellaneous collection of publications brought out by local authority housing departments and keeps files on about 30 of the local housing associations.

5 *Centre for Environmental Studies at the same address*
Shares library facilities with the HCT, and has collected a great deal of information in the general field since 1975. It has been widely used by many of those in the housing field listed below at the time this research was done, but has subsequently been moved to the Department of the Environment following the demise of the CES.

114

6 *The Institute of Housing, Victoria House, Southampton Row, London WC1B 4EB*
Organises study and research.

7 *Joint Centre for Regional Urban and Local Government Studies, J. G. Smith Building, University of Birmingham B15 2TT*
Formed in 1976 by a merger of the former Centre for Urban and Regional Studies and the Institute of Local Government Studies. The Joint library, containing about 40,000 items is mainly for the use of those doing courses and research at the Centre but is also open to outsiders. Its publications cover all the main general issues in the field. Pemberton's Report (p18) gives some details from the time he was writing.

8 *School for Advanced Urban Studies, Rodney Lodge, Grange Road, The University, Bristol BS8 4EA*
Set up in 1973 and covering a wider field than housing, SAUS contains a library of nearly 6000 books and pamphlets in the field and organises research and seminars. Its own publication list on 1st January 1980 had eleven items, together with a periodical.

9 *Capital Planning Information Limited, 12 Castle Street, Edinburgh EH2 3AT*
Formerly published *Housing digest*. Still brings out *Urbandoc news*, which is a monthly bibliography of urban and planning publications. Also provides the publications of a number of relevant research institutions.

10 *Housing Information Centre, 14 Queens Walk, London W5 1TP*
Produces *Housing abstracts* catering for the voluntary sector, mainly housing associations.

11 *Self-Help Housing Resource Library, Ladbrook House, Polytechnic of North London, Highbury Grove, London N5 2AD*
Maintains press cuttings, reports, official publications, pamphlets, leaflets, law reports, address lists and other such, mainly in the following fields: short life housing, squatting, housing cooperatives, self-building, tenant self-management, housing law, single person homelessness. Has a large collection on squatting, publishes bibliographies together with a good deal of duplicated pamphlet material and a periodical called *Self-help housing.*

12 *Research Library, Greater London Council, County Hall, London SE1 7PB*
Besides the services mentioned in Chapter Seven, generally for the use of those in the GLC and London Boroughs, the Intelligence Department produces a series of useful publications which are usually available to outsiders. Of general interest are the *Daily intelligence bulletin, Weekly Parliamentary bulletin, Committee reports bulletin, Borough intelligence newsletter,* a monthly summary of GLC and London

Borough research reports, *European digest* with information on the EEC. Of more specific interest to this project is the monthly *Urban abstracts* which is a monthly bulletin abstracting major articles from current journals, selected books, conferences and reports, constituting about 40% of what is received by the Research Library. This is said to be less comprehensive than the *Library bulletin* of the Department of the Environment, but fuller within its own field. The Library also produces a series called *Research bibliography*. Number 75 contains an annotated list of 56 references on *Sale of council houses* produced in May 1978, including statements by Government Ministers, pressure groups and others. Number 76, published in December 1976 contains 70 references to *Squatting*. More brief but similar information is provided in a series called *Reading list*. An example is three sheets published in September 1979 containing 42 references to *Homelessness,* mostly discussions of recent legislation. A series of occasional publications called *London topics* surveys more recent literature in a more general way. *Research memoranda* are generally of more limited interest and are actually thrown up by the work of the GLC's officers themselves.

13 *The Planning Exchange, 186 Bath Street, Glasgow G2 4HG*
This aims to pool information in a number of fields including housing for local authorities, other governmental agencies and interested bodies such as pressure groups. It issues a series of *Information bulletins*, listing publications, including a great number outside Scotland, all available through the Planning Exchange itself. It also publishes details of Scottish planning and appeal decisions, of its own forums, and research and occasional papers. Amongst other things, its library tries to stock 'semi-published material from local authority planning departments'.

14 *The Association of Housing Aid, 37a Waterloo Street, Birmingham B2 5TJ*
Publishes material of relevance to this field, including a regular *Bulletin* and a most useful *Directory of housing aid centres* 1979.

15 *Camden Housing Aid Centre, 83 Euston Road, London NW1 2RH*
Publishes a monthly *HAC abstracts* which summarises law reports, newspaper articles and many other items thought relevant to advisors including housing aid.

16 *National Federation of Housing Associations, 30-32 Southampton Street, London WC2E 7HE*
Publishes a monthly *Federation news* and keeps affiliates in contact with one another.

17 *Family Housing Association, 189a Old Brompton Road, London SW5 OAR*
Has a small library including official publications and the reports of other housing associations.

18 *The Library, Shelter National Campaign for the Homeless, 157 Waterloo Road, London SE1 8UV*

Press cuttings pamphlets and so forth arranged according to an internally generated numerical system. There are some general headings such as 5 for Aged, 7 for Census and 9 for Caravans. However, the vast majority are under 29 which is Housing. Thus 29-4 is Eviction, 29-4-2 is Eviction (public sector) and 29-21-11 is Rent Arrears. 29-21-4 is Housing Rent and Subsidies Bill and Act. This rather odd system seems to work reasonably well in situations where few if any enquiries are of a general character. Shelter produces the bi-monthly *Roof*, as well as numerous pamphlets, press releases and so forth.

19 *Information Officer, SHAC, 189a Old Brompton Road, London SW5 OAR*

The materials here are not so extensive, but logically organised under a series of colour codes covering a series of general topics. Blue is Poverty, Green is Housing, Red is Statistical and other guides, Yellow is London, Orange is Legal Matters, Mauve is Annual reports filed alphabetically, Pink is Government and Parliamentary Reports. Conferences and Acts and Bills are divided into their own separate sections. B5 is thus One Parent Families, G17 is Council Housing, G25 Battered Women, R10 GLC Annual Abstracts, Y6 Greater London Development Plan, 01 Legal Services. SHAC also publishes a series of Housing Aid Booklets, Research Reports and other pamphlets which appear in *The bookseller* and *British books in print*. These facilities are run by a qualified librarian, and material also goes to the copyright libraries.

20 *The Library, CHAR, Campaign for Single Homeless People, 27 John Adam Street, London WC2*

The material here is arranged under a series of numerical headings. 1 is Annual Reports (alphabetically); 2 Regional Reports; 3 Housing (eg 3.4 Housing in London); 4 Penal Reform; 5 Medical Care; 6 Homelessness; 7 Employment; 8 Social Policy; 9 Race; 10 Young People; 11 Women; 12 Government Pamphlets; 13 Acts of Parliament; 14 Statistics; 15 Bibliographies; 16 Miscellaneous; 17 Political Parties. CHAR produces popular one page 'Briefing Papers' on such issues as shorthold tenancies and the sale of council houses as well as leaflets on such issues as its efforts to close down Reception Centres. It also publishes more substantial pamphlets, usually in duplicated format surveying conditions and expressing its views on new legislation. A recent pamphlet in printed format published jointly with the Public Health Advisory Service is D. Ormandy and A. Davies *Standards of accommodation for single people* May 1977, outlines the present position and sets out proposals for the future.

21 *CHAS, Catholic Housing Aid Centre, 189a Old Brompton Road, London SW5 OAR*

117

This body has a small library, and to some extent shares information facilities with SHAC and the Family Housing Association, which occupy the same building. Besides its case work, it issues a number of publications in the field which all go to the British Library.

22 *Peterborough Central Library, Peterborough, Cambridgeshire PE1 1RX*
Issues packs of material, the housing one largely covering house buying and including leaflets from SHAC, the Building Societies Association and the local authority. The Citizens Advice Bureaux Files are also used. Further details on this and entries 23 and 24 can be found in Working Party on Community Information *Community information: what libraries can do* (Library Association 1980) Chapter Five, where there are also details of a number of other similar ventures.

23 *Longsight Branch Library, Stockport Road, Manchester M12 4NE*
The material here is largely arranged in boxes under a series of general headings. The concern here is more with 'social problems' though some of the written materials are of local significance only. The library relies a great deal on individual contacts, and also on liaison with local Citizens Advice Bureaux.

24 *Cheshire Information Service, c/o The County Council, Chester*
Organises a network of information centres throughout the county, working with libraries, tourist agencies etc.

25 *National Association of Citizens Advice Bureaux, 110 Drury Lane, London WC2B 5SW*
Sends out information files partly including official leaflets and partly objective accounts written especially. The material is divided into 14 categories and 11 is Housing, Property and Land, 11.0 is General, 11.1 Homelessness, 11.2 House Purchase/Home Sale, 11.3 Home Ownership, 11.4 Public Sector Housing (except Local Authorities), 11.5 Private Tenancies (eg 11.5.17 Rent Books), 11.6 Public Sector Housing (Local Authority eg 11.6.4 Rents), 11.7 Conservation and Land Use, 11.8 Town and Country Planning, 11.9 Rates, 11.10 Alternative Housing (eg 11.10.1 Mobile Home Parks and Sites (private)). These files are set up for the use of local bureaux, and though they are available to local public librarians and other professional users, they are not intended for consultation by untrained enquirers. The files are copyright and thus may not be reproduced without permission. The National Association hopes to improve this list of headings, which have been developed since 1974 as a result of consultation with experts in the respective fields.

26 *Publications Distribution Cooperative, 27 Clerkenwell Close, London EC1 0AT*
Specialise in the distribution of 'alternative' literature, mostly in book form.

118

27 *Scottish and Northern Books, Birchcliffe Centre, Hebden Bridge, West Yorkshire HX7 8DG*
Performs similar functions outside the metropolis.

28 *Grass Roots Bookshop, 1 Newton Street, Manchester M1 1RW*
Distributes and sells 'alternative' literature, including pamphlets, near print materials and other such. Publishes a 'Community Information Booklist' which included 23 items on housing, a few local. This is reproduced in *The radical bookseller* November 1979 p12.

29 *Campaign Books, West Library, Lofting Road, London N1*
Stocks materials from pressure groups and campaigning bodies, and issues a Community Communications Library Supply Catalogue, which under the heading Housing gives 37 items, some near print and similar material, largely from the well-known pressure groups.

30 *Coventry Workshop, 40 Binley Road, Coventry CV3 1JA*
The housing section of the library has, besides a few book and miscellaneous structure plans, a large number of files of newspaper cuttings, leaflets and so forth covering housing in the various areas of the city.

31 *Leeds Trades Union and Community Resource and Information Centre, 59 North Street, Leeds LS2 8JS*
Somewhat less material on housing, but rapidly expanding at the time of this research. See J. Haworth on 'The Community Library' in *Leeds TUCRIC bulletin*, 3 July/August 1978.

INDEX

Individual collections and organisations covered in the survey chapters and appendices are not included, except where they have a general significance for discussion in the book. Those items which occur too often to need to be noted separately include Ephemera and Printed Materials.